Imagination House
AN ENTREPRENEURIAL LIFE

E. LEE WALKER

Foreword by Will Wynn

TEXAS A&M UNIVERSITY PRESS   College Station

This paper meets the requirements
of ANSI/NISO Z39.48–1992 (Permanence of Paper).
Binding materials have been chosen for durability.
Manufactured in the United States of America

Library of Congress Cataloging-in-Publication Data Number:

Names: Walker, E. Lee, 1941– author.
Title: Imagination house : an entrepreneurial life / E. Lee Walker ;
    foreword by Will Wynn.
Description: First edition. | College Station : Texas A&M
    University Press, [2019] | Includes index.
Identifiers: LCCN 2019009551 (print) | LCCN 2019001565
    (ebook) | ISBN 9781623497842 (pbk. : alk. paper) | ISBN
    9781623497859 (ebook)
Subjects: LCSH: Walker, E. Lee, 1941– |
    Businessmen—Texas—Austin—Biography. | College
    teachers—Texas—Austin—Biography. |
    Philanthropists—Texas—Austin—Biography. | Dell, Michael,
    1965– | Dell Computer Corp.—History—20th century. |
    Computer industry—Texas—Austin—History.
Classification: LCC HC102.5.W345 A3 2019 (ebook) | LCC
HC102.5.W345 (print) |
    DDC 338.7/6213916092 [B] —dc23
LC record available at https://lccn.loc.gov/2019009551

To Jen

Contents

Foreword

In 1998, I was invited to a dinner party at businessman Sid
Galindo's apartment in downtown Austin. It consisted of a
dozen people who all seemed quite interested in—and ready
to work for—Austin's future. I was pleased to see that among
the guests was my new friend Lee Walker. Earlier that year
I had read an *Austin Business Journal* profile of Lee, the new
board chair of Capital Metro, Austin's public transportation
system, and decided that I needed to introduce myself to him.
The profile had mentioned that, like me, he had attended
Texas A&M, so we'd at least have something to talk about.
Then midway through dinner at Sid's I happened to overhear
Lee chuckle and mention a "ridiculous" decision he once
made while attending Harvard. He had taken a job in Africa
because Wayne Stark, a mentor of ours at Texas A&M, knew
a guy who knew a guy who had a cargo ship headed there.
Before Lee had completed his sentence, I had fallen out of my
chair onto Sid's floor.

Oh my God, you're *that* guy!!!

Let me back up a bit. Fifteen years earlier, when I was a
junior studying architecture at Texas A&M, I knew of, but
had never met, the director emeritus of the Memorial Student
Center, Wayne Stark. Mr. Stark maintained an office on
campus, and I took it upon myself to make an appointment to
meet him. I knew that he had served as a mentor of sorts to
hundreds of college students over the decades, and I was just
smart enough to guess that I needed help thinking about my
upcoming and final year of college, not to mention what the
hell to do with myself after that.

Mr. Stark had convincing opinions about things a laugh-ably myopic young person like me should do immediately if I wanted to make something of myself. But mostly he simply told stories about other students that he had mentored and what they had decided to do and what had become of them. His most common story, and obviously one of his favorites, was about some young "two-county boy" ("Just like you, Will," he said) whom he had helped get into Harvard Business School but who had somehow ended up on a random cargo ship headed to some obscure place in Africa. By this late stage in his life, some of the details of Mr. Stark's oft-repeated stories dif-fered slightly, shall we say. But I spent as much time as I could that year quietly listening and absorbing more than I knew.

So by the time I had graduated and (convinced by Mr. Stark) had moved to Chicago—*Chicago*?!?!—I had pieced together a fairly elaborate (and largely invented) image/story of this faceless predecessor of mine. I couldn't remember his name, maybe never knew it, but the story—and Mr. Stark's fondness for it—would, for the next decade or more, randomly cross my mind. And I would find myself asking, "What would *that* two-county boy do in a situation like this?"

The reason I was even invited to Sid Galindo's dinner party in 1998 was because I had recently quit a very good job in the commercial real estate development industry so I could focus on my passion of promoting mixed-use urban projects in downtown Austin. As a point of reference, in 1998 Sid was one of about 400 people who actually lived in downtown Aus-tin. And approximately 320 of those 400 resided in the Travis County jail!

I also wanted to get more civically involved. I wanted to be in a position to better promote my vision of a new urban dynamic for Austin that included people living, working, and playing in very close proximity, a bunch of "environmental

urbanists." And I was the incoming chairman of the then-
obscure organization later known as the Downtown Austin
Alliance.

I left Sid Galindo's dinner party that night still shaking my
head at the incredible serendipity of my realization that my
new friend Lee Walker had in fact already been an inspiration
or guide, of sorts, for me for the previous fifteen years. And
I suspected—and hoped—that now there was a lot more to
come. And I was right.

Lee and I worked closely together on so many projects,
starting with coproducing a public television series called
Austin 2000. We conspired on both a losing and a winning
urban rail election. Winning is more fun. And with Lee's
help and encouragement, in between rail elections I was
elected mayor of Austin. I still can't decide whether *that* was
fun or not.

But one definitely fun exercise as mayor was cutting
through a morass of municipal red tape enabling Lee's
cohorts at the Sustainable Food Center to launch the remark-
ably successful downtown farmers' market in Republic
Square. That perfectly complemented my goal of convincing
thousands of residents to live downtown. And at 11:00 p.m.
one night—literally the eleventh hour of the failing labor
negotiations needed to avoid a midnight strike by Capital
Metro's bus drivers—Lee pulled up to the corner of Fifth and
West Avenue in his big pickup truck. I hopped in so he could
drop me off at the airport hotel where the union leaders and
labor negotiators were at a standoff. I simply played late-night
messenger for Lee's final offer that broke the stalemate. I was
publicly acclaimed as a brilliant mediator and savior. I just
knew to trust that two-county boy who once stowed away on a
cargo ship headed to Africa.

Here in this book Lee tells many stories. What I find

fascinating is that a number of these "lessons" occurred years after Wayne Stark, my college/life advisor, used Lee Walker as the personification of stories that I needed to pay attention to. In retrospect, I was a "student" of Lee Walker's long before he even realized that he was a teacher. And once I connected the dots at Sid Galindo's dinner party, I also realized that my adventure in lifelong learning, continually inspired by Lee, was just getting started.

WILL WYNN
Former mayor of Austin, Texas

Preface

Two summers ago I was in torment.

I was driving home in an unhappy frame of mind along Italy's Lake Trasimeno. I had just given what I thought was a poor talk in Castiglion Fiorentino, a small city in eastern Tuscany where a group of incoming Texas A&M University freshmen were doing an orientation to their study abroad program. In my misery, I realized that I had to stop inflicting myself on these trapped students. I had been giving this talk about my life as an entrepreneur for the last eight years. The time had come to stop this annual tradition of mine.

Was this how old baseball pitchers felt when they realized they had lost their speed and accuracy, when they were washed up? Was this how they felt when it was time to check out and retire? As I drove the confusing dark road that threads through the Antognolla Valley in Umbria, I tried to concentrate my seventy-three-year-old eyes. No sense compounding my misery by hitting a tree or going over the edge into the next valley below. Somewhere along that narrow winding roadway, an idea began to form.

Suppose I wrote a little book that captured what I wanted to say. Suppose my audience got the book in advance. Suppose all I had to do in the future was show up and be a sweet old man willing and ready to have a chat with students.

Would that idea work? Because if it did, maybe I would be asked back in the future. Maybe for many years, maybe till I was 100. The world might not need another book, but oh my, did I need one.

As I turned into the last little valley that leads to my home, my spirits lifted as that small book began to take shape.

Imagination House

Introduction

I was looking for a way out.

As a boy walking barefoot along the dusty streets of Three Rivers, Texas, I wondered if there didn't have to be more, but I didn't know what "more" might mean. I thought something must be missing, but I had no idea what that might be.

My mind searched for an escape from the arid sameness of each day and for relief from the South Texas heat in a time before air conditioning. It was the 1950s, what writer Elmer Kelton called "the time it never rained," a time when it was drier in some parts of Texas than during the great drought of the Dust Bowl era. My hometown of 1,900 people was no different from other rural communities, in some respects a great place to grow up, but there wasn't a whole lot going on beyond Friday night football and church on Sunday.

In the summer of 1952, soon after I turned eleven years old, our family began subscribing to a newspaper for the first time. My dad, who worked as a chemist at the local refinery, had gotten a pay increase to $7,000 per year and must have thought we could now afford this luxury. I hadn't known about major league baseball before the morning paper dropped into my life. I was fascinated by numbers, and the statistics and the box scores on the sports page of the *Corpus Christi Caller-Times* mesmerized me.

Baseball, its teams and their history, was an exciting and new way for me to learn more about the world. Soon I wanted to know the dimensions of every major league ballpark in the country. I learned how idiosyncratic the shape of each one was from a book I ordered through the mail. I memorized each park's dimensions, making scale-model outlines on the floor of my bedroom, especially intrigued with the peculiar geometries of Fenway Park, the Polo Grounds, and Ebbets Field. These parks were in cities I'd never heard of before: Cincinnati, Cleveland, and Brooklyn.

I learned about "the shot heard 'round the world"—Bobby Thomson's home run in the bottom of the ninth inning that won the National League Pennant for the New York Giants at the Polo Grounds in 1951. The Polo Grounds looked like a lopsided bathtub of a field, a relic from its historic past when it opened in 1890. It measured 257 feet down the right-field line, 480 feet to dead center, 279 feet to left field. A little pop fly could be a home run, a titanic swat to center just another out. I was dumbfounded that Thomson's historic home run would have been an out anywhere else, and the good people of Brooklyn wouldn't have had their hearts ripped out one more time. Then it happened again in 1954 when the Cleveland Indians, my favorite team, lost in the Polo Grounds because of its peculiar shape.

Was this where my obsession began about how our places shape our lives? Did our destinies depend on the shape of our places? Did mine?

Before my family moved to Three Rivers, we lived in Missouri and in Kansas, where I was born. When I was six, I found a set of red books in the basement of our house. The basement was creepy; the concrete floor bore a permanent blood stain from the previous owner, who had taken his own life there. But my fear was no match for my fascination with the red books. I stroked their pale red faux leather covers, studied their maps, dreamed about the faraway places they described.

I didn't know where the red books came from. I noticed they were printed in 1941, the year I was born. I wondered

if God had put the books in the basement for me. No one
else seemed to know or care about them. I ran my forefinger
down the still-joined perforations at the edges of the pages to
separate them, astonished and pleased that no one had opened
them before.

I wondered if it was a sin to make marks on the maps.
I supposed it was probably at least a venial sin to tear the
maps out and take them to bed with me for further study by
flashlight. But I knew I hadn't reached the age of reason yet;
Catholic Church teaching was clear on this point. Technically
I wasn't capable of committing a mortal sin until age seven.
Since I was still six years old, I knew a loophole when I saw
one. I didn't need to confess anything to anybody. By the
time my family moved to Three Rivers when I was ten, I had
studied and restudied my red books, less and less worried
that anyone else would notice or care about those missing
maps. My thirty-volume set of *Encyclopedia Americana* was
my magic carpet to ideas and places far, far away.

On October 4, 1957, the front page of the *Caller-Times*
announced the Russian launch of Sputnik, the first human-
made Earth satellite. I was a junior in high school, amazed
that the Russians had beaten us to the punch, flabbergasted
that we couldn't respond. Our rockets just sat on the launch
pad fizzling or they exploded. I became obsessed with design-
ing, building, and launching my own rockets.

I wasn't the only person experimenting with rockets in
response to Sputnik's challenge. Enough people had been
seriously hurt from their experiments that the U.S. government was putting out information warning which chemicals
to avoid. These warnings about what to stay away from were
a treasure trove of ideas for me, describing the prohibited
chemicals and combinations that I would not have discovered otherwise. My launching pad was a couple hundred

yards down the hill from our house, through a dense thicket of cacti and mesquite trees. One gorgeous Sunday morning, after many scary failures, I watched the first successful liftoff of one of my rockets in a brilliant burst of a green-colored cloud. When I walked back up the slope to my house, I saw my mother twisting the skirt of her apron at our back door.

After I graduated from high school, I went to work as a roustabout in the White Creek oil lease near Simmons, Texas. I figured it would take only two or three years to save enough to go to college somewhere. But I caught a break when I was recruited by Texas A&M to play basketball on a full scholarship. During my senior year I was featured in a full-page story in a national edition of *The Sporting News*, whose headline read, "Missile Man Launches Orbiting Aggies." The accompanying photo showed me, the six-foot-nine center for the Texas A&M team, reading a Russian newspaper while getting ready for a big game.

The Russian language had become something of a mind-calming refuge for me. I buried myself in the poetry of Anna Akhmatova, tales by Mikhail Lermontov and Ivan Turgenev, the stories of Leo Tolstoy. In Tolstoy's epic *War and Peace*, Prince Andrei dreams of glory. He knows that Napoleon Bonaparte was a nobody until he commanded a siege of Toulon, France, in 1793 that defeated the British. Without Toulon, Napoleon said, he would have been just another artillery captain in the army.

Prince Andrei is obsessed with gaining fame when his Toulon moment comes along. In the Battle of Borodino he recklessly charges up a hill, is wounded from a mortar shell, and dies soon after in almost total obscurity.

When I first arrived at A&M, it didn't take me long to realize that I was going to sit on the end of the bench in

almost total anonymity for four long years. Our star player
was going to be Lewie Qualls, a seven-foot-tall high school All
American. And that's the way it was until early in our senior
season in 1962. We were playing Tulane University. Lewie
was having an off night, so Coach Rogers put me in. I played
well, then followed that with another good game. Coach
announced I was the new starting center, and when I continued to play well, the Texas press began to write me up. *The
Sporting News* picked up my story not long after and made me
look like a big star.

It's difficult for anyone not from that geographical place or
from that era in time to understand what a big deal the South-
west Conference used to be. Whether Prince Andrei would
have understood, I don't know, but in the sports context of
that particular time and place, the game against Tulane was
my Toulon moment.

Since my daily schedule was made up of going to my physics, math, and Russian classes, sweating through brutally long
basketball practices, all before returning to my room to study
until early morning, the idea of any extracurricular activity was
impossible. I did make one exception when I joined the Texas
A&M Russian Club and was elected president. (There were
five of us in the club. I voted against myself, but only one other
person joined me.) I thought it would be fun if we watched
Russian films, but where might these be found in the middle
of conservative Texas in the midst of the Cold War? No one
could tell me, but I was told that if anyone knew, it would be
Wayne Stark, the director of the Texas A&M Memorial Student
Center (MSC).

I walked over to meet Mr. Stark. From the moment I
ducked through his office door I sensed something was going
on. His office was in the basement of the MSC at the far end
of a long, low corridor. He instantly had time for me, wanting

to know everything about my background. I didn't realize that he was drawn to guys like me, timid small-town boys with barely developed notions about anything.

He helped me find the Russian films, and when my dad died three weeks later from lymphatic cancer, Mr. Stark was to become my fail-safe supporter, my biggest booster. He had several mantras, all of which struck me as quirky and counterintuitive. He thought I should read the liberal *New York Times* every day. He believed I should attend plays and operas on a regular basis. He recommended that I begin to plan to live and work in as many foreign cultures as possible. He also thought I should attend Harvard Business School.

Some of these ideas struck me as unrealistic, others not remotely interesting. But Mr. Stark was persistent, and I soon became a follower of his advice. There is no question that he filled an emotional void for me, and I drew closer to him. Over time I began to understand that Wayne Stark had a particular specialty. His stock in trade was collecting and telling stories. His delectation over a good story was akin to the pleasure of an epicure over a great meal.

By the time Wayne Stark died in 1993, I had gone to Harvard Business School, launched my own companies (some were successful, others were not), become the first president of Dell Computer Corporation, and left the corporate world to become a college professor. By the early 1990s, it was clear that with the success of Dell Computer, something special had been created in the marketplace. Even today, Dell's imaginative enterprise model is studied in business schools around the world. Mr. Stark was hungry for details about how we had pulled this off, and because I was a creation of his, he took a proprietary pleasure in the smallest details.

The stories that follow are told in a way that I believe Mr. Stark would have wanted me to tell them. I include a fair amount about the emergence of Dell Computer because I know that's what he wanted me to talk about the most.

I can hear him whispering in my ear, "Be sure you don't leave anything out."

CHAPTER 1

It Began Because of Baseball

Jim Seymour telephoned on the spur of the moment, inviting me to dinner. As luck would have it, I was available. I wasn't very busy in those days. He thought I would enjoy meeting Michael Dell, the computer wunderkind who had just turned twenty-one. According to Seymour, Michael was about to hire the first president of his two-year-old personal computer company. The new president was from Brooklyn.

Seymour was an early evangelist of the personal computer industry, writing columns for *PC Magazine* and *PC Week*. He was an influential, trusted advisor to many, noted for his skill in making sense of complex technology and business issues. Jim spoke at a velocity that made many of us wonder if he defined some upper limit, a sort of Seymour 1.0, a speed beyond which no other human could speak.

We met in a private dining room at Beijing's, a new restaurant in northwest Austin. Smacking his lips, Seymour suggested sesame chicken, the specialty of the house. Michael and Jim sat at one end of an oblong table. Jim was talking a blue streak; Michael was silent.

The man from Brooklyn—I don't recall his name—and I sat at the other end of the table. I guessed my job was to earn my supper by asking him lots of questions, but not necessarily chitchatting about computers. I knew what I wanted to ask him. What I wanted to know was whether he had ever seen the Brooklyn Dodgers play. Yes, he'd been to many games at Ebbets Field when he was a child. He saw Carl Furillo gun down runners from right field, Duke Snider hammer home runs, and Jackie Robinson steal home, driving pitchers crazy.

My mind's eye skated to that time. I saw old-fashioned flannel uniforms with royal blue Bs flapping in the afternoon sun. I had never met anyone who had actually been to what I considered that holiest of holy places, Ebbets Field. It had been destroyed by the wrecker's ball more than twenty-five years before, when the Dodgers abandoned Brooklyn, uprooting to move to Los Angeles, and before I understood baseball was a business, not a holy cause.

When I was growing up in South Texas in the 1950s, I tried to beat the heat of a great seven-year drought by lying on our tile floor, my ear plugged in to our brown enamel radio. My favorites were adventure shows like *Straight Arrow* and *The Lone Ranger* and live-broadcast baseball games. Fidgeting with the dial, I listened to Harry Caray and Gabby Street calling the play-by-play while etching the landmark numbers of baseball into my brain: Joe DiMaggio's 56, Babe Ruth's 60, and Lou Gehrig's 2,130.

Over dinner at Beijing's that April evening in 1986, the Dodger I wanted to know most about was Carl Furillo, nicknamed "the Reading Rifle" from his days playing minor league ball in Reading, Pennsylvania, before going to Brooklyn. He was also called "Skoonj," from the Italian word *scungilli*, which means snail. It was a tip of the hat to his Sicilian roots, his slowness of foot, and the toughness of his skull, as it seemed he was always getting beaned, hit in the head by opposing pitchers.

I was full of questions for the man from Brooklyn.

"Was his throwing arm as great as they say?"

"Yes."

"How did he play balls off that right field wall?"

"Just about perfect."

"Didn't he once throw out a runner at first base after fielding his line drive on one hop?"

My dinner companion said yes, although he never saw it happen himself. He said usually it had been a slow runner, like a pitcher. I asked him if he remembered Furillo's lifetime batting average. He said no.

"Wasn't it .299? And Duke Snider's lifetime batting average, wasn't that .295?"

"I don't remember."

"Damn, I often thought it was a minor tragedy, because I'm pretty sure Furillo was one hit shy of .300. Funny thing about reaching the .300 level, it's not a guaranteed ticket into the Hall of Fame, but it's such an important milestone. If he had gotten one more stinking hit, a little blooper, I wonder if he wouldn't have been voted into the Hall of Fame. Just one more Texas Leaguer in all those thousands of times at bat."

I'd overdone it. My dinner partner was looking away, worn out or bored by my obsession with the Dodgers and Furillo.

Later that evening, Seymour, Michael, and I stood outside in the parking lot. Seymour wanted to know my impression of the man from Brooklyn.

"He seems like a good guy. I like him, but how could he grow up in Brooklyn and not know the lifetime batting average of Carl Furillo?" I asked in disbelief.

Seymour's face began to turn red. "Walker, it upsets me when you give frivolous answers to serious questions."

"Seymour, if you don't want my opinion, why ask for it?" We wheeled and stomped away from each other.

Several years earlier I had met a different Jim Seymour. I had recently moved to Austin, and I was doing research at my business partner's law library on an investment we'd made. My back was to the door, and a gigantic arm reached across me to get a book. I turned around and saw the biggest person I'd ever seen. He told me he was getting a law book to do research on a case. I asked him if that's what he did for work. "I live by my wits," he said. He told me he was a writer, a photographer, a musician—there was nothing he wasn't.

"So tell me," I asked, "how are you doing?"

"Terrible," Seymour said. "I don't know how I'm going to make my mortgage payment this month."

I was just instantly taken with him. At the time I had a number of companies in the northern part of the country, and I worried that someday I wouldn't be able to remember the details of what I'd done. I proposed to take Seymour to photograph all of my companies. I had a shortening company in Chicago that supplied the Keebler cookie and cracker company's shortening. I had a nuclear metallurgical laboratory where we made americium dioxide pellets for smoke detectors. And I had a specialty valve company and a medical products company. These companies were the result of my entrepreneurial career, which, Lord knows, was spotted with numerous false starts and mistakes.

"I'll pay for your travel. You charge me a fair price for your work," I said, and Jim agreed. He came away from that trip thinking that I was not only a good businessman but an unusually agile entrepreneur. From that point forward Jim was bonded to me because I'd helped him out in a pivotal moment.

Driving home from Beijing's years later, I was rattled. Seymour had thought he'd done me a favor by inviting me to meet Michael, and he expected me to behave. More than that, he had wanted to big dog it a little bit, showing the influence he now wielded. And I had gone off on some side street of sports trivia. What I should have done was enjoy my free meal, smile at Seymour's power game, and go home without incident.

But I hadn't because there was a part of me that couldn't.

Carl Furillo was then a sixty-three-year-old security guard for a company in Pennsylvania. He was the forgotten Dodger from those mythical teams that had won one National League Championship after another. He was a demigod who had fought his heroic struggles in a historic place that was no longer a place.

What I didn't know that night was that Carl Furillo had only three years remaining before his death from a broken heart. What his doctor called a heart attack.

Suppose Furillo had had one fewer times at bat. Maybe one less hitless at bat would have given him a .300 lifetime batting average. Maybe his life was a lesson on the importance of knowing when to quit, quitting in time, quitting when you were still ahead.

Pulling up to my home on Cat Mountain, I tried to comfort myself by musing that nothing important had happened. This evening would soon be forgotten.

I was wrong, as I was about to discover.

CHAPTER 2

An Unexpected Request

"Would you be president of my company?"

I looked up from my sandwich. Michael Dell had shown up uninvited at my front door a few minutes before as I was sitting down to lunch. I asked if he was hungry. He said yes, sat down, and began shoveling food down in that way I used to eat when I was twenty-one, as if any meal might be my last. Michael's drop-in visit was a surprise in view of my nuttiness at Beijing's a few days earlier.

I told him no, that we were leaving soon, in a few weeks. We'd be gone for the summer. My first wife, Mary, and I had found a home in France's Loire Valley to rent for the summer. During an internship in Africa twenty years earlier, I had decided to learn French since three of the countries I would be working in were former French colonies, Morocco, Tunisia, and Algeria in particular. But I had learned almost nothing despite intensive lessons. There was something about the French language that seemed unnatural to me, counterintuitive, too subtle and nuanced for my South Texas tongue and brain. I decided that I hadn't worked hard enough then to learn French. This time would be different.

Michael chewed his sandwich and slurped some soup. "Okay then, would you be president for a few weeks?"

I didn't know what to say. Should I ask what happened to the man from Brooklyn? Or why me, this bit of a burnt-out case who had come home to Texas eight years earlier in 1978?

"Michael . . . it's Michael, not Mike, right? You're from Houston?"

I realized I knew almost nothing about him. How could he know much about me? He knew I liked baseball statistics, but what else? None of this made any sense. You don't go around asking people to be president of your company without vetting them first.

Michael began to describe his life growing up in Houston, his early days of making money in stamp collecting and delivering newspapers. I had once been a stamp collector and, at six foot nine, had been possibly the world's tallest newsboy when working my way through graduate school at Harvard by delivering the *Boston Globe*, the *New York Times*, and the *Wall Street Journal*.

Michael told me about his enrolling at the University of Texas, about the beginnings of his computer business in his dorm room, about his parents' disapproval, and then about his scrambling to hide his inventory of parts in a friend's room whenever his parents popped into town. When he couldn't contain his computer compulsions any longer, he told his mom and dad that he was quitting school so he could devote himself to his business full time.

That had happened two years earlier. Now he needed help.

"Let's take a walk," I said.

On the pine needle pathways in the Ashe juniper woods on the east side of Cat Mountain, I showed him my favorite lookout places—where I sat in the morning to watch the sunrise, and the crumbling gazebo, where I watched the sun set every evening like an old man waiting out the rest of his days. (Though only forty-four, I was already a month older than my dad, Dallas, was when he died from lymphatic cancer.)

The year 1986 was a tough time to be trying to do what Michael was trying to do. Money was drying up in Austin. Pools of investment capital were evaporating. Texas oil and land prices were imploding. There were rumblings of big bank problems in our town; the five largest were teetering. Even John Connally, my fellow South Texan from Floresville, the man nearly killed during the Kennedy assassination, the thirty-ninth governor of Texas, and the former US secretary of the treasury—even he was declaring bankruptcy.

I had moved to Austin because of my decision to grow old there, a decision I had made back when I first visited the city as a high school student competing in a statewide slide rule competition (think Stone Age calculator) at the University of Texas. I was taken in by the seeming sophistication of the university's Gregory Gym with its glass basketball backboards and the city's abundance of libraries. By the time I moved to Austin in 1978, the city's expansion into the growing technology market was beginning to take hold.

I am predisposed toward technology. It represents change, which I inherently like. My interior programming seems to love its complexity, its possibilities, its capacity to give access to regular people and upset the established order. But my own forays into Austin's technology companies hadn't panned out. I had tried to help Balcones Computer Corporation, but it collapsed. I had tried to help in the formation of Factorial Systems, a software company, but it had missed the mark. I was on a losing streak.

When I first moved back to Austin, I had wondered about a company called Balcones Computer Corporation from the moment I heard it was manufacturing all of the personal computers for the government of the state of Texas. With that strong base of business, it seemed as if it could be one of the survivors as the number of players in the PC industry began to whittle down. I couldn't figure out its business model, so when the company asked me to join its board of directors, I jumped at the chance. Attorney Dick Baker and I had helped form an early venture capital firm in Austin. Dick had gotten to know me as we analyzed many prospective investments. I guess he liked my decision making, because when Balcones was looking to create its first board of directors, Dick, the company's attorney, recommended my joining the board.

I was baffled by Balcones' business model, and I thought maybe as an insider I would gain an understanding as I immersed myself in the company's strategy. I love puzzles, and I wanted to figure this one out. I also hoped I could help refine the business model going forward.

In our initial board meeting I had an opportunity to examine my board book for the first time. I went straight to the financial statements, with no less attention to the balance sheet than the income statements. One of the hardest things for new ventures is to manage their money in an effective way. In my view, Balcones Computer was an almost textbook example of this difficulty. My reaction was immediate. While Balcones had done nothing wrong, I feared the company was in serious financial trouble, and I didn't want there to be any confusion as to where the responsibility lay for what I believed was a mess. I apologized, saying I had to resign immediately.

But I am programmed to try to help out. I thought I could be most helpful if I remained a totally independent outsider. In the weeks and months that followed I tried to help the management make sense of their situation. Frank Phillips was president of Texas Commerce Bank (TCB), the same bank that held Balcones' loan. Frank once told me that his secret was to listen carefully to what his customers wanted and how they wanted to receive the help they needed. Then he did his best to give them what they needed the way they wanted it. Frank told me that if Balcones' $1.5 million loan was not repaid, it would be TCB's biggest loss since Braniff, an international airlines company that was one of TCB's biggest clients. In the 1970s Braniff was the company of the moment: it painted its planes in unusual colors, and the flight attendants dressed provocatively in outfits by top designers like Pucci. I regarded Frank Phillips as one of the great men of Austin and wanted to help him. I also wanted to help Balcones Computer by serving as an honest broker between the company and its bank.

In time the great effort and ingenuity of the Balcones management team found a way for full repayment. Acting as a trusted intermediary, I helped out when final negotiations were going on, running room to room as a settlement was reached. Frank Phillips must have been terrified that the bank was going to lose its entire loan amount to Balcones Computer because he was surprised and delighted that TCB received its entire $1.5 million back.

I had also served as chair of Factorial, a start-up software company. Factorial had made a deal with Tandem Computer to sell and install its combination of software and hardware to companies wanting to radically upgrade their manufacturing efficiency. We at Factorial didn't realize that our deal with Tandem was not an exclusive one: Other companies could also sell their manufacturing systems. This vastly undermined our strength in the marketplace. We also didn't realize that we had the right to sell only a portion of the manufacturing system, which further undermined our prospects. We had an incomplete business model. This incompleteness was fatal. It seemed that this insufficient due diligence on my part was a recurring pattern of mine, that I wasn't as good a businessman as I projected myself to be.

As Michael and I continued on our walk, I thought back to February 1972. I was living with Mary at 74 Irving Place in Buffalo, New York. One morning at 4:00 a.m., I had woken up in a full-scale panic attack. My teeth were banging up and down against one another. Shivering, sweating, suffocating,

I had thrown off the comforter that was smothering me. This wasn't a dream. I had lost all my money, all my investors' money. And it took only two weeks. I thought at the time that that must be a record for bankruptcy.

My secret would soon be out all over town. I felt like Texas sucker bait, trying to play businessman in Yankee land. A thirty-year-old imbecile trying to be a big shot. A damn fool. Why had I trusted that man? Because he wore a tie and was over ninety years old, and his name was Walter?

No sense in trying to get back to sleep. I dressed in the dark without waking Mary. I tiptoed down the stairs, out the front door, and down slippery steps to my 1968 green Dodge Dart at the curb, crusted over with a half inch of Lake Erie ice.

I hadn't told anybody anything. I knew the moment I spoke of my failure, the words would be alive in the air. And once my words were in the air, they'd pass over my backyard fence to one of my investors, John Fisher, who lived directly behind me on Park Street, then ricochet down Delaware Avenue to my attorney and investor, Vic Raiser, flop over to my banker, Bill Wilson at Manufacturers and Traders Trust on Main Street, and flip to another investor, David Rumsey at Marine Midland Trust, the guy who brought me this disaster deal in the first place.

I drove slowly west on North Street toward Canada (Why not Canada? Haven't others taken refuge there?) and then onto Porter Avenue with the crunch of old snow under my tires. I tried to piece together what had happened.

It had looked like a good deal, maybe a great deal. The owner of Kellogg Mann Corporation was a ninety-four-year-old man who wanted to sell his incinerator company. During our negotiations, I thought he was also looking for a surrogate son to pass his business to. Since I had lost my father to cancer ten years earlier, I was ready to be Walter's progeny.

And I was ready for a life of profitable entrepreneurship after five years of postgraduate apprenticeship working for Union Carbide, a Fortune 500 corporation.

Walter was tall and gruff. He wore boots, a suit, and a tie, and carried himself with near-perfect posture, what I wanted to look like someday. Truth was, I wanted to believe: wanted to believe in him, wanted to believe I could be an entrepreneur, and wanted to believe he held the ticket to my escape from corporate life, which felt stifling. I wanted to control my schedule, how I invested my life. My projection onto Walter blinded me to the red flags that he was cheating me, pure and simple.

What had I missed? Was there a telling detail? Turns out it had been right in front of me. When I first visited Kellogg Mann's office, I had seen cups, saucers, and buckets scattered about on desks, chairs, filing cabinets, and the floor. I later learned they were there to collect rain dripping from the leaking roof. Had I gotten up on the roof, I would have realized how lax this company was in maintaining basic standards. I saw only what I wanted to see.

And I had a big idea. Garbage to energy.

I thought this was the perfect fit for me, to have a company that helped the environment by saving energy. There are at least 5,000 British thermal units of energy hiding and locked away in every pound of garbage. It would be pretty simple to hook up a waste heat boiler to an incinerator behind every store, then plow that energy right back into the place that produced the trash. In Buffalo that would be wonderful warmth to ward off the epic winters that bury it under prodigious piles of snow. No messy containers in the back, no haul-away expenses, no landfill charges.

And I believed that one day the prices of oil, $3.50 a barrel in 1972, and gasoline, then 35 cents a gallon at the pump, were going to jump. When that price leap happened, my heat-reclamation products would catapult off the shelves. I'd be more than rich, I'd be the prescient genius who saw the future before others did.

Things went well at the deal closing. Walter wanted $90,000 for his business. I could only raise $30,000. Walter was willing to take back a note for $60,000, further evidence of our close personal connection and his belief in me and in the future that I would build on the foundation he had begun. After the closing, I drove over to Kellogg Mann's drab little office, a mottled and faded lime cinder block building at 361 Dewitt Street directly across from the Coronation of the Blessed Virgin Mary Catholic Church.

There were six employees, none of them paid very much, and one seemed especially unhappy from my first day of work. Then I found out why.

He wept as he told me that all of our products were illegal: all of them had failed the New York State environmental standards. He had falsified the results because Walter demanded he do so. Like me, this employee had found Walter's character impossible to resist. The man was clear that if we continued to sell and install our products, we would be knowingly breaking the law. I looked through the office's glass partitions at the faces of the other employees. Their shamed, downcast eyes confirmed their colleague's awful truth.

I walked outside and into a Buffalo snowstorm, got into my Dodge Dart, drove slowly home, and curled into a fetal ball of misery and confusion.

Once upon a time, I had been headed for a life in physics research and teaching, the kind of academic activities that appealed to the gentler side of my nature. But when my father died, somehow the physics thing slipped away, and business and commerce invaded my days.

I came out of my reverie and turned to Michael Dell as we walked back around Cat Mountain. "I can't help you. I'm sorry."

We shook hands, and he left. As he drove away, I thought again about my own beginnings in business, how desperate I had been for help, and how I had almost gone under. When I was starting out, I made every possible mistake. There was so much I didn't know. And I had no sense of the number of people out there waiting to cheat and devour one another, me included.

If I hadn't known much about these things when I was thirty-one, how could Michael know them at twenty-one? I had two college degrees. He was a dropout. I was sad. Michael needed a mentor, but I was mentored out.

CHAPTER 3

The Pivot

"We want you to stay away from Dell."

I looked up from a plateful of chicken enchiladas drenched in Fonda San Miguel's exquisite mole sauce. So this was why I had been called and invited to lunch. MBank didn't want me anywhere near Michael Dell's company.

MBank was one of the three largest banks in town, having been established in 1890 as American National Bank of Austin. In 1984 it became MBank. Its distinctive headquarters glowed in sunlight as if its outside walls had been painted with luminescent gold, prompting one friend to say, "Ain't they supposed to keep the gold inside their safe?" As it turned out, MBank would file for bankruptcy, collapsing one year before its 100th birthday. But on this day the bank was buying my lunch.

The MBank loan officer across the table from me had graduated from Texas A&M University and the University of Texas with finance and accounting degrees. While I didn't know him well, we had done a bit of business in the past, and I held him in high regard.

Earlier, when driving over to the restaurant, I had wondered if he was going to ask me to write a check to the United Way or join the Chamber of Commerce. So, if this was all he wanted, I was getting a free lunch, better yet a free lunch from one of the best restaurants in Austin. In his own way, he was asking that I keep on doing the nothing I was doing, the nothing I was planning on doing anyway.

There was no reason for me to cross-examine him. If MBank didn't want me around, it didn't want me around. Good enough. Maybe someday I might want to borrow some money from MBank, so I might as well keep this conversation light, enjoy my meal, and pile up a few reciprocity brownie points. The guy had made his sale to me and should have stopped talking.

But he didn't.

He began to describe his admiration for an Austin company called CompuAdd. He said MBank was CompuAdd's bank as well as Michael Dell's. While I had never heard of CompuAdd, I wasn't about to admit my ignorance.

He explained how CompuAdd had precisely the same business model that Dell did, selling directly to its customers, how CompuAdd was larger and much more profitable, and how it had better systems and was more professionally managed. In the survival shakeout of PC companies, he thought CompuAdd would make it. He didn't think Michael Dell would.

"Lee, you may not know it, but we've frozen Dell's credit line at $600,000."

I did some mental math. I remembered Jim Seymour had told me that Michael's sales were about $100,000 a day. That meant MBank was financing only about six days of sales. My rule of thumb gleaned from hard years of experience was that you need funding for at least twenty-four days of sales. Six days, $600,000, was impossible. MBank had decided to put its boot down on Dell's financial windpipe. Michael's suppliers had to be way past due in getting paid. And they must be kicking down his doors, screaming for their money.

I sighed and said I wanted to skip dessert and coffee. Our lunch quickly came to a close. As I got into my car and sat for a while, I thought back to 1972 and that frozen February morning in Buffalo when I had been desperate for help. Beyond desperate, I had been sinking fast and flailing with no help in sight. My dream had been destroyed, not by a bank but by a ninety-four-year-old man. And it would have been all over for me if a friend had not invited me out to lunch to celebrate my beginnings as an entrepreneur.

When I had first moved to Buffalo in 1970, I discovered a city that was shrinking in population, a city with many abandoned buildings, a city where entrepreneurship seemed the exception, not the rule. Those of us who considered ourselves entrepreneurial were well aware of one another because there were so few of us.

One of those few was a thirty-one-year-old Buffalonian named Taylor Kew, who owned and operated his own business, a steel coil handling manufacturing operation. It was Taylor who would casually mention the idea that ended up saving me. (One of my regrets in life is that Taylor died before I could tell him how central his help had been to me, how completely he had affected my life.)

When Taylor had taken me out to lunch in what he thought was a celebration of my start-up business, he said he wished he had the money to buy a local steel fabrication business that was closing down because of mismanagement. Taylor believed that in the right hands it presented a great opportunity. Since he wasn't going to pursue it, he hoped I would take a look.

I had always planned at some point to go into manufacturing because of my deep-seated belief in the importance of making one's own products. In the past the Kellogg Mann Corporation had always outsourced all of its production. I believed that someday my new company would need to manufacture its own products, and, when it did, the very act of making them would stimulate creativity in new product designs, ideas, and breakthroughs.

After meeting with Taylor Kew I decided to visit Universal

Metal Welding, the company he had mentioned. By chance
I caught the owner just as he was pulling out of an empty
parking lot in his white Lincoln Continental. If I had arrived
even two minutes later, I would have missed him entirely. It
didn't take long for the two of us to hit it off before he offered
to sell me his business, adding the inducement that he would
finance almost all of the purchase price, a pivotal point since
I had lost all of my money on Kellogg Mann.

When Bill Wilson of Manufacturers and Traders Trust
Bank said he would provide the financing I needed as well
as lend me additional funds for the working capital, I had a
path forward. That help I received from my bank was in stark
contrast to the attitude of Michael Dell's bank.

But even with the essential help of Taylor Kew's offhanded
brainstorm, the generous terms I received from Universal
Metal Welding's owner, and the abundant support I got from
my bank, I was far from out of danger.

A potentially fatal problem developed when a key customer
announced that he was not going to pay me for an installation
we had just made in Tampa Bay. I flew to Tallahassee in complete panic and awoke the next morning to witness a historic
event.

"We are honored to have had the opportunity to serve our
country under difficult circumstances."

I moved closer to the black-and-white TV set in my motel
room, squinting at the men behind the speaker, Admiral
Jeremiah Denton. I searched the faces of the men standing
behind the admiral. There. That one. Could it be him, my
friend and former Texas A&M classmate Jim Ray?

Eight years had passed since we were last together at
one of our weekend culture trips in Houston, arranged by
our mentor Wayne Stark. Jim had spent the past almost six
years in Hoa Lo, a prison dubbed the Hanoi Hilton, in North
Vietnam after his F-105 was shot down on May 8, 1966. Now

at long last a war that seemed to have no end—the Vietnam War—was over, and my friend Jim, Admiral Jeremiah Denton, John McCain, and other POWs were free to come home.

"Difficult circumstances." Earlier that morning I had thought my circumstances were difficult. I had flown to Tallahassee to convince the Florida Department of Environmental Regulation (DER) to allow my customer in Tampa Bay to use a reclamation furnace my company had built and installed. If we didn't get a waiver, we didn't get paid.

The product in question was a new one we had developed at Kellogg Mann and was built by our new subsidiary Universal Metal Welding since we could no longer sell our existing products using the old, illegal technology. This new technology took advantage of the differing melting points of tin, lead, and copper in reclamation from scrap metal. This product was a big-ticket item with a high gross margin, a good deal for our customers and a good deal for us. Assuming we got paid.

I stood in line, waiting to speak in front of the DER's chairman and board members. Those of us in line were allowed three minutes per appeal. I watched as attorneys made their company's requests. The three-person board turned down every single one.

When it was my turn, I gave my remarks. The chairman turned to his right, then to his left, nodding to each. He delivered their verdict: request denied.

"Mr. Walker, please step away from the podium." Instead I gripped it with both hands.

"Mr. Walker," he said again, "please step away from the podium."

In that moment I think I forgot about being scared. I began to talk almost without thinking. I told them that if I stepped away from the podium, that step would be my first one toward returning home to a bankrupt company. If the

Florida DER didn't give me a variance, my customer wouldn't pay me. I was a small businessman who barely scraped by month to month. The future of my little business was at stake. I had installed a recycling furnace whose purpose was to help the environment. I begged the DER to reconsider.

The chairman looked to his right, then to his left. "Okay, we've changed our decision. Permission granted."

I wobbled outside and slumped to the floor. I was shocked at the arbitrary life-and-death power this governmental unit had over my business. I was stunned at how close I had come to ruin. And how had I, someone so fond of conflict avoidance, found the courage to protest the committee's decision? I know it had felt quite emotional seeing Jim Ray on television earlier that morning. Perhaps seeing Jim and his fellow POWs had emboldened me, although clearly our situations were incomparable. Although my new business still dealt with the normal issues all new businesses face, from the Tallahassee event forward my business seemed to break free.

As I sat in the parking lot of Fonda San Miguel after my lunch with MBank's loan officer, it seemed to me my early days were a distant echo of what Michael Dell was experiencing in 1986.

I understood that a bank might feel uncomfortable lending money to a twenty-one-year-old college dropout in a business with no barriers to entry and a flood of new competition every week. So why had the bank lent money to him in the first place? Well, whatever the reason had been, it was clamping down on the oxygen supply now.

I started my car and headed west toward the home of my friend and neighbor Ron Carroll. Ron was one of the smartest businessmen I knew, a savant with a deep dossier of who was doing what to whom in Austin. If anyone could help me sort things out, Ron was the man.

CHAPTER 4

The Millionaire Ice Back

Ron Carroll was a millionaire "ice back." When I first met him, he lived as an "illegal immigrant" in an ultrachic home at the base of the east side of Cat Mountain. Born in Toronto, he was an undocumented CEO working in the United States and an avid collector of antique automobiles, including a vintage 1930s maroon, leather-bodied Packard, a Duesenberg, and a Bentley, all in pristine condition. His garage was larger than my house. His company, Continuum, traded on the NASDAQ exchange and provided software and technical support for global insurance companies.

From time to time, Ron had to travel outside of the United States on business or to visit his relatives in Toronto. In the years before 9/11, leaving the United States wasn't hard. But getting back in without documentation? That was tricky. Ron would book a first-class seat from Toronto to the island of Montserrat, where he owned a vacation home. His flight would make a brief stop at JFK Airport in New York City, where he would step off the plane to stretch his legs. And then walk away.

His luggage and personal effects? He'd shipped those earlier to his home in Austin. The airlines never figured out this eccentric man's pattern of behavior, someone who only occasionally made it all the way to Montserrat.

Finally, after massive legal fees and many years of persistent effort, Ron had become a US citizen. Our hometown of Austin was slightly diminished, a little less weird, now that one of our most prominent businessmen no longer needed to sneak in and out of the country.

Ron lived directly below my home, a short walk down through the woods of Cat Mountain. I was drawn to him from the moment we first met. He had the look of a recluse, a shy loner. As I had gotten to know him, I was stunned at the degree of his shyness. He made me feel like a wild party boy. Ron's manner seemed standoffish: his body language implied that he didn't want physical contact. So from our second meeting I made it my habit to give him a gentle hug every time I saw him. As it turned out, he was on the lip of a divorce and later would tell me about his black depressions during that time.

When Ron was home, he usually was in his garage hunkered under the hood, tinkering with one of his cars. That day I was lucky. As I walked through the woods to his house, I saw that Ron had just pulled in, still wearing his roadster cap and looking like an English squire who had come in from the fox hunt.

As we walked up Cat Mountain Drive, I told Ron about meeting Michael Dell at Beijing's (leaving out the Carl Furillo part). I then told him about Michael's visit to my house, about his asking me to become president of his company, about my refusal, and finally about the luncheon with the loan officer at MBank.

In his soft-voiced Canadian accent, Ron told me he saw no problem: I didn't want to join Dell, the bank didn't want me to join Dell, and, most important, the prospects for Dell were so poor that it was a bad idea anyway. Ron did have a certain genius for making succinct summations. But the mini mystery of why MBank didn't want me getting involved still remained.

High above us turkey vultures funneled in wide arcs, their

six-foot wingspans catching the uplift from Cat Mountain. I knew their roost was just beyond the ravine to our right, a spot they had probably occupied for a long time. There were so many of them that day I wondered if they were an omen of some kind.

Ron said he had three ideas (his fertile imagination seemed to always serve up multiple scenarios for any question). He had a raspy voice, and when he spoke he was convinced he was quite funny. He would punctuate his sentences with a kind of glottal chuckling wheeze, inviting others to enjoy his hilarity. In retrospect, I think his distinctive throaty sound was a symptom of the lung disease that would be diagnosed two years later and eventually take his life.

Ron's first theory was that I had butchered the last two companies I had been involved with, Balcones Computer and Factorial Systems, a couple of early Austin technology startups. Ron said that perhaps the bank thought I was a menace to anything I touched, but his crooked smile told me he was yanking my chain.

While I knew Ron wasn't serious, I had to go through the motions of defending myself. I pointed out that Balcones Computer was insolvent before I first walked in the door. I had helped to clean up the mess, including helping its bank, Texas Commerce, get its entire $1.5 million loan back. Regarding Balcones Computer Corporation, I was blameless.

But Ron's Factorial Systems criticism had some bite to it. I had thought that Factorial's technology, created and licensed by Tandem Computers, would help companies make their manufacturing operations much more efficient. Ron pounced on that argument. He said that most of the world except me knew that manufacturing was history in the United States. Ron was partly right: At that time in the mid 1980s, the popular argument was that labor costs were too high to continue manufacturing in the United States. Japan was in its ascendancy, and its manufacturing quality was superior to anything made stateside, so it made good business sense to outsource manufacturing operations.

I did love the idea of we Americans making our own stuff, and I probably did get carried away with my belief that we needed to manufacture more things in our country. In any event both Ron and I knew that nothing he had said had anything to do with why MBank didn't want me around.

Ron's second theory was that Michael Dell's company didn't have a chance against the likes of IBM and Compaq, and the bank knew it. Michael's company had a capital base of $1,000, and in a broke town he couldn't raise any more money. As a company PC's Limited had no sophisticated operating systems while trying to compete against huge enterprises with great economies of scale. Michael's company had no patents and was infringing on the proprietary technology of IBM in particular. According to Ron, IBM would soon pull the plug on all clone companies that were encroaching on its patents and products.

By 1986 MBank's officers saw this clearly. They understood that at best one or two of these clone companies would emerge, but they didn't believe PC's Limited was going to be one of them. In fact, the loan officer had said as much during our lunch when he spoke admiringly about CompuAdd. MBank had taken the first step away from supporting PC's Limited, which was freezing Michael Dell's line of credit. Soon they would demand full repayment. They wanted their $600,000 back—no muss, no fuss, and no delay. Ron thought maybe MBank was worried that if I got involved it would be harder for them to close things down.

While I agreed that MBank's officers wanted their money back, I didn't think they were worried that I would gum up their plans. I watched Ron as he pooched out his generous lower lip, gathering his thoughts as he got ready to tell me what he thought was going on. He started by asking me if I knew that the banker I had had lunch with and Michael Dell's CFO were best buddies and might have gone to school together. I shook my head. Then Ron asked me if I knew that Dell's chief financial officer and chief accounting officer were married. That piece of news was a complete surprise. Talk about amateur hour. There was no way you could have that lack of check and balance in your financial setup.

Then Ron landed his knockout punch. "Lee, the bank is bankrupt. MBank is going down." He explained how with their bad real estate loans on top of their nonperforming oil loans, the bank was headed into insolvency. It was in a mess that would take years to clean up. Ron thought that the smart insiders knew the bank was going bankrupt. And they knew they needed to be looking for their next job.

None of this had remotely crossed my mind. Ron's imagination, which leaned toward the conspiratorial, went into high gear. He spun a web of intrigue in which the banker, the CFO, and the CAO were plotting to put Michael's company into receivership, then, out of a reorganization, take it over. So the banker didn't want me around because I would sniff out this scheme and, with my Catholic altar boy sense of fairness, help Michael thwart their plan. Even worse, I would figure out where to get money to screw up their plans. What a wicked imagination my friend had. No wonder he had made so much money.

Ron and I knew about Moore's Law—that processor speed would double every two years. We shared a belief in the impending shakeout within the PC industry. For me, it was mostly informed by my constant discussions with Jim Seymour. For Ron, it was from his perch as one of Austin's seminal software pioneers. But Ron had something that

Seymour, the technology writer, didn't have: years of experience as an executive. Imagination was important, but execution was what ultimately mattered, and this was at the heart of Ron's objection to my getting involved with PC's Limited. He valued my creativity and my entrepreneurial drive. In fact, Ron had invited me to join the board of directors for his software company Continuum, which I did, and then he had relied on me during negotiations when he sold Continuum to Computer Science Corporation in what became, at the time, the largest acquisition in Austin's business history. But Ron thought of me as more of a book-loving intellectual than a CEO. I had run companies, of course, but they had been small to mid-size businesses. And if Ron was evaluating my executive abilities based solely on my involvement with Factorial and Balcones, then he might assume I didn't have the executive chops to help lead Michael Dell's company.

During those volatile days in the early computer industry, fledgling companies like PC's Limited needed all the help they could get. Computer giants like IBM and Compaq sold through retail stores partly because buying a personal computer was such a big and complicated investment. IBM introduced its personal computer in 1981 at chain stores, including ComputerLand and Computer City. Just like in the automobile industry, computer companies embraced the commonly held belief that customers needed stores so that they could see, touch, and try out the product—take it for a test drive, essentially—and then feel good about spending several thousand dollars to buy one.

This was the conventional wisdom at the time, and even Michael Dell hoped to one day open PC's Limited retail stores. In 1986, however, he and other PC clone competitors were jockeying for position in the market by selling direct to those buyers willing to purchase their personal computers over the telephone. The commonly held belief was that direct sales could never exceed more than a small percentage of market share, and this is the reason that so many business analysts were skeptical that PC's Limited could ever be a big player in the larger computer market.

This was a decade or so before the Internet began to take off, and buying something as expensive as a computer sight unseen was considered a risky venture. But selling direct—what seemed like a limitation for Michael Dell in 1986—eventually would become one of the key factors that set his company apart.

Walking back to my house through the woods of Cat Mountain, I knew Ron hadn't solved the puzzle I had brought to him. I still didn't know why MBank didn't want me around PC's Limited. If anything, Ron had only added to its complexity with his various theories.

Because I am cursed with the need to solve any puzzle before me, I was frustrated with the lack of resolution. Irrespective of MBank's motivations, Ron had been helpful in giving me additional reasons for staying away from PC's Limited. In sum, he thought it was a hopeless mess that I should avoid so as not to add to my list of failures. In any event I had heard enough from my wise old friend Ron Carroll, a trusted colleague for many years, to stand firm on my rejection of the offer from Michael Dell, someone by comparison I barely knew.

CHAPTER 5

Day One

No way am I doing this.

Driving to PC's Limited on my first day of work, I wondered: How did I get from "no way am I doing this" to "hi ho, hi ho, it's off to work I go"? I had called Michael Dell after changing my mind and asked him to meet me at the restaurant Chez Zee in northwest Austin. Over coffee and cherry pie, I told him I'd do my best to help out.

I didn't know what a fair deal would be and didn't want to be taking advantage of his being in a bind, so I suggested that our friend Jim Seymour propose what my pay should be. (I felt a little guilty taking anything when Michael's credit line was frozen at the bank, and money was in such short supply.)

Why did I change my mind? I thought the Dell matter was dead and done after my long walk up and down Cat Mountain with Ron Carroll. Michael's company didn't seem to have much of a chance. Besides, my family and I had been planning to leave town for the summer.

So why did I change my mind?

Somehow while shaving one morning I did a full 180-degree turn. I wasn't even thinking of Michael or much of anything while keeping an eye on my parrot, Chelsea, who was perched on a towel draped over my bare right shoulder, her head bobbing as I scraped my face.

Amazon green, Chelsea was a passionate parrot. Whenever she began to dilate and contract her pupils (eye pinning, it's called), I knew she was getting "het up." Usually I could swivel my head in time to avoid her love bites. But not always.

My wounds were never deep, but why did I put up with Chelsea? For openers she seemed to love me a lot. Plus, she was brilliant. It was fun to sing with her. Our favorite duet was from Ivan Susanin's aria in the last act of *A Life for the Tsar*.

I had taught Chelsea how to sing in Russian so that I could continue to practice speaking the language that had captivated me since college. During my sophomore year I took Russian 201 and made my first visit to Professor Skrivanek's office. He didn't like to shake hands—too many germs might be on my giant hands. His immaculate fingernails were trimmed and neat; his fingertips were pink with constant scrubbing. I noticed a book on the top shelf behind him, *The Complete Works of Anna Akhmatova*. I asked if I could borrow it.

He took it down, removed some loose, handwritten pages from within, and asked that I return it within three days. He didn't want to be without it very long. I took it back to my dorm room and began to read.

> В узких каналах уже не струится-
> Стынет вода.
> Здесь никогда ничего не случится,
> О, никогда!
> Может быть, лучше, что Я не стала
> вашей женой.

Oh my. This language was surely the most perfect for poetry ever invented by mankind. It filled my mouth as if I had stuffed it with roasted chestnuts, cracked open, warm, and chewy, such that every part of my mouth was suffused, satiated by Cyrillic sounds.

> узких
> каналах

уже
может
лучше
вашей
женой

My expatriate Russian friend, Dmitri, said he missed terribly the physicality of the Russian language fullness that flooded him. ик, ах, уж, ож, уч, ше, аш, же, ой—these sounds filled him, and their absence made him ache with longing. I continued to leaf through the book and came across another poem, translating it into English:

You will hear thunder and remember me,
and think: she wanted storms. The rim
of the sky will be the colour of hard crimson,
and your heart, as it was then, will be on fire.
That day in Moscow, it will all come true,
when, for the last time, I take my leave,
and hasten to the heights that I have longed for
leaving my shadow still to be with you.

I was undone. I was in love. I began to send off applications to every possible avenue that might get me to Russia.

After all, I was the president of the Texas A&M Russian Club. Dr. Skrivanek had pushed me to do this because he loved that I was a star basketball player, and he could come to our home games and cheer me on. I could see him in the stands during our warm-ups, his coiffed hair glowing silver in the midst of Aggie crew cuts.

Every day by mail my Russian newspaper, *Novoye Russkiye Slovo*, arrived. I looked in vain for snippets of news about Anna Akhmatova. But somehow this newspaper didn't regard her as newsworthy.

As president of the Russian Club, I had to find films we could watch. Finding Russian films during the Cold War in the middle of Texas was not easy, but I met a man who helped me get a copy of the black-and-white classic *Alexander Nevsky*.

Then, great news! A scholarship from the student-exchange program Experiment in International Living was offered to me, allowing me to live with a family in Russia for the summer. In Leningrad, only 25 kilometers from Anna's home at Tsarskoye Selo.

I shifted into high gear, cramming an hour a night with my book of Russian grammar. I would find Anna. Dr. Skrivanek told me I had a distinct, clear Leningrad accent, except he said a "St. Petersburg" accent because he refused to acknowledge the Soviet's name change.

Then came disaster. Nikita Khrushschev, the leader of the Soviet Socialist Republic, suddenly slammed the door on any Americans visiting Russia. He was angry about the loss of face in having to back down and remove his missiles from Cuba. I walked straightaway to the Eastgate Bar to drown my sorrows in bottles of Pearl beer.

A few days later, another letter arrived.

"Dear Mr. Walker," it said, "your scholarship is still valid." How about another communist country, another Slavic place? How about the land of the southern Slavs, Yugoslavia? A family, the Pavlovics, awaited me. They had read about my basketball exploits and wanted me to live with them in their small, simple apartment in Novi Sad near the Danube River. I could go there, get settled, maybe slip away for a tryst with my beloved Anna.

It did not happen. I did get to Novi Sad and spent the summer chasing around Yugoslavia while learning to drink Slivovitz, their lethal plum brandy. But there was no opportunity to leave for Russia. When I first crossed the border by

train from Greece into Yugoslavia that summer, the border guards kept my passport and wouldn't return it. I was
trapped in Yugoslavia until my passport reappeared at the
end of summer on the day of my departure back to the West.

After returning to Texas, I began work on my PhD in
cosmic physics, still burning with the hope of meeting Anna.
I called my friends at the Experiment in International Living.
Was there any possibility of an opening? Maybe I could lead a
group to someplace near Anna's home in northern Russia?

By then Anna was seventy-five. She had been constantly
persecuted by the Soviet authorities. Because of a chance
encounter she had with Isaiah Berlin in Leningrad, they
thought she was a spy. They had met in 1945, when Berlin
was the first secretary at the British Embassy.

How much longer did Anna have? I needed to try once
more.

Sweden was just across the Baltic Sea from my Anna. I
was told there might be an opening for a leader of a student
group going to Sweden in the summer of 1965. There were
a couple of problems, though. First, I was too young to be a
leader. You had to be at least thirty; I was twenty-three. Second, I knew no Swedish. A leader to Sweden had to be fluent.
So I bought a Swedish language book and began to study.

I then learned the founding mothers of the Experiment
in International Living were meeting soon for a leadership
retreat in St. Louis, Missouri. And bus fare to St. Louis from
College Station and back was cheap.

I arrived in St. Louis wearing a rumpled suit after a 760-
mile bus ride. I found the hotel where the women were staying,
and I sent a note up to them introducing myself, hoping they
would meet me. They had a better idea. They were taking a
cruise that evening on a Mississippi steamboat. There would
be dinner and a dance, all informal. Would I like to join them?

I put aside my shyness and my aversion to dancing. I did my best to smooth my travel-worn suit, and I added a long, dark tie. (I didn't know how to tie a tie, but my teammate Chuck McGuire did, so I kept the preknotted tie he made for me on a hanger and packed it for the trip.) That evening, with no idea how to dance, I sat with the ladies and asked each of them if they would dance with me. They were all tiny, wizened, frail. They tittered at my offer, saying yes. It was a sight no doubt: me, six foot nine, twenty-three, and them, five foot nothing, average age of sixty- or seventy-something or other. I told them the trip to Sweden was terribly important to me. I might have even suggested it could be terribly important to Anna. I oversold them on my gift for languages, driven by my passion about meeting Anna.

I was back home in Texas for just about ten days when a letter arrived from the Experiment in International Living. Would I be willing to accept a leadership position for a student group going to Sweden? My answer was yes.

That summer in Sweden was brutal. I rode a motor scooter from village to village, looking after ten American high schoolers living with ten different Swedish families. Sweden's driving laws were like England's then, and I frequently wound up driving on the right (actually, wrong) side of the road, having to careen into a field to avoid crashing head on with another driver. I had to stay in close watch of the students, and I did not have the time (or money) to ferry across the Baltic Sea to Leningrad. Still no Anna.

Upon my return to Texas, I decided to drop nuclear physics. I entered Harvard Business School and was soon buried in a strange world preoccupied with money and commerce.

On the morning of March 5, 1966, I glanced at a copy of the *New York Times*. I had run out of time. The headline read:

Anna Akhmatova Dead at 77
Heart Attack

Many years later, I had taught my parrot Chelsea to sing the
beginning of Susanin's lament in a perfect St. Petersburg
accent: "чуют правду," which means "they suspect the truth."
(The Russian peasant hero is about to be murdered by the
Poles because he has tricked them, leading them away from
the first tsar in the 300-year Romanov line of succession, the
young boy Michael I.)

And when I was shaving with her on my shoulder that
morning in May 1986, my epiphany came out of the blue.
"I'm going to leave town for the summer, knowing what I
know, and when I return in September, Michael Dell may
have lost his company. If I had stayed and helped, well, who
knows what would have happened."

I felt a stab of pain in my right cheek and saw a red trace of
blood seeping through the white lather. Chelsea was flapping her wings, triumphant. I walked her over to her regular
perching place, dabbed off the remaining shaving cream, and
put a piece of Kleenex on my cheek to staunch the bleeding.

I then went to the phone and called Michael Dell.

We met later that morning at Chez Zee. I don't remember much of what we said. I think I compared our situation
to being on a sailing ship of olden days, with lots of piratical
characters swashbuckling around us. Michael and I would
have to cover each other's backs in complete trust as we dueled
multiple adversaries. I said I would do my best to be helpful as
long as I could, recognizing I had now passed the number of
days my dad had lived before he died at age forty-four.

On the first day, I pulled into the parking lot in front
of industrial gray Building Three at 1611 Headway Circle,

painted with horizontal stripes of pastel red and blue. I parked my car, kept the engine idling, and sat, reflecting in those last quiet moments.

I knew the first thing I had to do from my discussion with Michael. I had to fire the chief financial officer of Michael's company. The reason had nothing to do with Ron Carroll's wild conspiracy theory. Michael was simply unhappy that this officer had not been able to obtain sufficient funding for the company.

He and Michael had recently argued about something, and Michael was so upset that he had stormed away, slamming his office door behind him, not realizing that his CFO was close behind, still wanting to say more. The door jammed the CFO's foot against the door frame. While nothing was broken, the CFO was now on crutches. My first act as the new president of Michael's company was to fire someone hobbling around on crutches.

I didn't like firing people. I remembered the first man I had ever fired, some eighteen years before, when I was one year out of school. He was a sweet middle-aged man who peeled his wire-rim glasses off after I broke the news to him, put his forehead down on my desk, and began to weep soft, racking sobs, his bald head bobbing up and down.

Now this morning, I was about to fire someone on crutches. Then after I fired him, Michael wanted me to fire that man's wife, the chief accounting officer.

I got out of my car and trudged up the steps of Building Three.

It was only day one.

CHAPTER 6

The Head Coach of Tandem

I stared at the certified letter addressed to me, which required that I acknowledge receipt. It was from Bob Swem, plant manager of the local Tandem Computers, Inc.

Mr. Swem's tone was menacing as he asserted that we were poaching on Tandem personnel by luring them to PC's Limited. After a few words of boilerplate about how we were violating state and federal statutes, Mr. Swem made his central point: We needed to stop hiring Tandem employees. Or else.

They were reserving their rights to press claims against our company—and me personally—for our "tortuous inter-ference" into their business. (I looked up *tortuous*, loving its tangled complexity.) Swem continued that we had already seriously harmed his company and that they were evaluat-ing the extent of damage in preparing to bring legal action against our company and me.

He again demanded that we stop doing what we were doing before closing the letter with the hint that a nasty letter would soon follow and the implication that this letter was by comparison a little love tap.

—o—

We were having a rough day.

It was the fall of 1986, and I had been president of PC's Limited for only a few months. A customer from Des Moines, Iowa, had just called, warning me that he was on his speaker phone recording our conversation and that he had his attor-neys with him in close attention.

"Are you the president of this so-called computer company?" he shouted.

Without waiting for a reply, he began yelling that one of our computers had exploded in his bedroom, starting a fire that was contained only by the grace of God and the Des Moines fire department. As a result of this "explosion and conflagration," his home-based business had been irreparably harmed, and he intended to sue both PC's Limited and me. Moreover, he was in touch with the Better Business Bureau of Austin, where he had learned that he was but one of many who had been damaged by our "lousy computer firebombs."

"I'm going to break you bastards in two," he screamed. "Treble damages for interstate fraud," he shrieked.

So we had issues.

We had just finished our fiscal year with $33 million in sales. We were on a pace to double it that year. But 100 percent hypergrowth was straining our limited manufacturing capacity and quality control.

We were in danger of becoming the next Osborne Computer, a company that earned more than $100 million in sales before imploding and disappearing into the PC history books alongside the scores of dead and dying companies that were going under as IBM and Compaq turned the thumbscrews of price and quality.

We needed some fundamental fixes, and we needed them soon. Our problem was that fundamental fixes took time and money. We had neither.

Despite our problems, people were flocking to our door looking for jobs.

The economy in Austin was a wreck, destroyed by the twin pile drivers of a horrendous real estate bust on top of the devastation from plummeting crude oil prices. Most Austin companies were struggling. Within the tech industry, employees of Data General Corporation, Digital Equipment

Corporation, and even Tandem were beginning to look around and see issues with their companies' business models. But PC's Limited seemed to be an up-and-coming place, and jobs were scarce. But we offered more than a job. They could sense something exciting was happening. PC's Limited may have been financially strapped, but it was a workplace that practically glowed with energy and enthusiasm. Maybe they could also see themselves as a bigger fish in a smaller pond. We offered potential job security in the high-stakes game of personal computers.

The threatening letter I had received from Bob Swem at Tandem had some basis in fact. A number of Tandem employees had contacted us, and we had hired a few of them. We hadn't recruited them, and this was still America. If someone wanted to leave a company and go to work for another company, that was his or her right.

But we only had a thousand dollars of capital on our balance sheet. We were vulnerable. A one-foot-high tidal wave could swamp us.

The man who was mad in Des Moines and the angry plant manager from Tandem needed calming down, not to mention the other product quality complaints we were wrestling with. We just weren't strong enough to withstand an onslaught of lawsuits.

What to do? My sense of the right triage was to turn my attention to doing some research on Mr. Bob Swem. What was his story?

As I asked around, I discovered a trove of information about him. The more I learned, the more intrigued I became about the possibilities that might be hidden within this dilemma.

Bob Swem was a fifty-year-old manager of the Tandem Computers plant in North Austin. Before his job at Tandem,

Bob had worked at Data General. For him, Data General had been sheer hell, like working in a penitentiary. He had hated his time there. What a mistake it had been for him to join a company that discouraged employees from hanging out together, taking too much time for lunch. It was a company that, in his opinion, went beyond frugality to soul-killing cheapness.

However, Tandem Computers was an almost perfect match for Bob. He managed the factory that made its terminals. Tandem terminals were the faces of its fault-tolerant computer systems, systems that were nonstop, ultrareliable. Banks, stock exchanges, and ATMs needed fault-tolerant, failsafe computer systems of the highest quality. And Tandem Computers dominated these markets.

Bob Swem was born and raised in Wichita, Kansas, not far from where I was born in Coffeyville. He worked while going to night school at Wichita State University, majoring in physics. He crapped out when he hit quantum mechanics. "I couldn't figure out Schrödinger's Equation," he said.

Some people want to be doctors, teachers, writers. Bob's ultimate aspiration had always been to be a plant manager. To Bob, being a plant manager was like being the head coach of a place that made something. And the place couldn't just be anywhere. It had to be a plant somewhere west of the Mississippi River. He often said, "There are too many people who behave like jerks east of the Mississippi."

Bob Swem wanted every terminal made in his plant to be of the highest quality and to have its own identity. He wanted every terminal made in his plant to be the responsibility of one person, and he wanted that person's name on the terminal. When a broker on Wall Street was making his millions using his Tandem terminal, that broker needed to see Suzi Smith's name right up front on the terminal. Bob wanted there to be a connection between the user and the maker. He wanted to get away from the nameless, faceless way of making things that Henry Ford had established in the 1920s with his mass production philosophy.

It was a romantic idea, perhaps, that the Wall Street millionaire would come to feel a connection with the person whose name was on the device that was his primary working tool. Perhaps one day this Wall Street titan would be in Austin, Texas, and would take time to go out on the Tandem factory floor to personally thank the Suzi Smith who, in fact, had helped him make his millions.

Bob Swem told all the Suzi Smiths that even when you have shipped the product out the door, it's still your responsibility. If it ever comes back, you have to fix it. You own it for life.

But Bob got into an argument with his boss, a vice president with Tandem. Bob wanted to spend an extra $1.50 per terminal to get labels with signatures on them, one signature per label. These labels would tell the world who was responsible for each individual terminal. Bob was certain the pride of authorship and quality that would flow from that signed ownership would far outweigh the incremental cost of $1.50. Bob's boss disagreed, vetoing the idea. Bob said screw it and went ahead and did it anyway, easily hiding the costs in one of his side pocket accounts.

Another aspect of Bob's innovation was giving each individual part within each product its own unique identity. Every capacitor, every resistor, every subpart of every product was bar-coded so that every part's life trajectory could be tracked.

Bob had been refining this idea for more than ten years, even before his time with Data General, back when he was still working for NCR in Wichita, Kansas.

Bob was obsessed with being able to track an order from the moment it began its life on the factory floor to the time it was shipped and, if need be, to the time it should ever come back.

Bob knew that he could submit all of his products to continuous testing to find out what parts were the first to fail under rigorous burn-in. So if a 50-watt capacitor was the first thing to destruct, then all customers with 50-watt capacitors could be contacted, and each would receive upgrades with 100-watt capacitors so they wouldn't fail in the field. If fail-safe, reliable, nonstop fault-tolerant systems meant the highest possible quality, it meant proactive replacement of key parts before those parts could fail in the field.

This was an almost perfect meshing of a company, Tandem, and a personal philosophy, Bob's. Almost perfect. Even closer to perfect was still waiting in the future.

—◦—

I'm not sure when Michael and I hatched the "big idea." It was probably while driving over to Tandem's plant where Bob Swem was waiting for us.

Michael and I had now worked together for a few months. We discovered that we fit well together. Both of us were naturally curious, analytical, and biased toward immediate action. And we trusted each other. We kept the door between our offices open so we could hear one another and pop in to juggle whatever was burning.

Something was burning. I knew Michael had heard the man from Des Moines screaming about what awful arsonists we were. And Michael knew better than anyone the fragility of our situation and the importance of fixing our systems as soon as possible. Bob Swem's letter helped spark the idea.

Michael and I were ushered into Bob Swem's office. He shook our hands and was cordial, showing no signs of the testiness that his letter had conveyed.

Since Bob was from Kansas, I knew there was no reason

to do the normal Texas foreplay of beating around the bush looking for connection. We got right to it and sprang the "big idea" even before it was fully formed. We had a proposition for Bob to consider. Rather than going down the legal path with its wasteful expense of time and money, why didn't we cooperate?

Why didn't we buy a clutch of Tandem Computers to run our plant, using Tandem's ultrareliable systems to ensure that we were never down? Why didn't we take precisely the same exquisite system that Bob Swem had invented and put it in our place so that we could track all our orders and subparts in precise real time? Why didn't we use our place as a show-case for Tandem Computers and Bob's shop-floor system?

Essentially, we were proposing that a giant skyhook reach down, take the Tandem manufacturing hardware and soft-ware system model, lift it gently to the sky, carefully move it a few miles south to our place, and softly lower it on top of our operation, where it could be fully exploited.

In exchange for this, we would stop looking at any more job seekers from Tandem. Even better, we would welcome prospective Tandem customers who might want to visit us to see the true power of Tandem hardware in combination with Bob's elegant and robust manufacturing system.

What we knew, but didn't say outright, was PC's Limited would go from last place to first place in product quality—if he would only say yes.

Bob Swem was silent. He seemed to understand well what we were proposing.

I looked into his face. I wondered if he would be large enough to get past the normal issues that bedevil us men, the issues of wounded pride, a need for dominance, an instinctive desire to lash out against those others who we think are doing or have done us wrong. Could he get past any fears of looking weak, fears of making a mistake, fears that his bosses might second-guess him?

I closed our conversation with a cliché right out of those western movies I loved as a boy, some of which were set in old-time Wichita itself. "Bob, I want your answer by sundown."

Later that evening, my home phone rang as the sun was setting to the west of Cat Mountain.

Bob Swem was on the line. "Lee, are you willing to make a handshake deal on what you proposed?" I said yes.

Our verbal handshake soon turned into reality. Our plant quickly became a model for how to make PCs, indeed anything. While we weren't able to implement the Suzi Smith name label, we were able to designate every order, every computer with its own distinction, its own particular identity.

The power of Bob's system had never been fully unleashed at Tandem because of the relative lack of variety in terminals. But in our case there were infinitely many variations of features any individual PC might contain. Our made-to-order PC concept was close to a perfect fit with Bob's made-to-order tracking system.

It was as if Bob had been in the unpaid hire of PC's Limited in the ten years plus that he had spent developing his manufacturing approach. In time, PC's Limited was to become near the center of reimagining how things could be made. Our plant floor model became the stuff of legend, a classic Harvard Business School case study of how a company could dominate its industry through its manufacturing techniques—thanks to Bob Swem, a man from Kansas who wanted only to be the head coach of a place that made something west of the Mississippi.

CHAPTER 7

International Expansion

"We do it, we go bankrupt."

"No, we won't. We gotta do it."

Cradling Earth in one arm, Michael pointed his forefinger at England on the inflatable plastic globe he was holding. He then chest-passed it back to me across our board of directors table.

We never sat during our two-man board of directors meetings but walked in a clockwise direction around the table that also served as our guest meeting table, weekly sales staff meeting table, our all-purpose table for any gathering of any kind. We couldn't sit still. There was way too much adventure in the air.

I grabbed Michael's pass, twirled it Harlem Globetrotters style, then returned it with a flourish behind my back. Not too much deterioration since my ball-playing days at Texas A&M.

Michael caught the world, almost two feet in diameter, its oceans acrylic blue under the fluorescent ceiling lights. He finger-walked across the Atlantic Ocean and again pressed his forefinger deep into England, arching his right eyebrow, nodding his head to reinforce his message. "Look, we gotta do this . . ."

"We can't," I said. "And something else we can't do is open any stores."

The balloon ball came whiffling straight at my head. We started walking faster, not quite trotting around the table. I muscled the world right back at him as hard as I could.

Michael stopped and perched the planet Earth on his forehead, tilting his head back, extending his arms straight down, showing off his circus seal balancing skills. It was a diversionary move to get me chuckling, to make me lose focus. That wasn't difficult. The sillier things got, the more susceptible I was to manipulation, especially if Michael went into his Inspector Clouseau impersonation: "You fool, I want a room."

Maybe Michael was right about our need to get going internationally as soon as possible. But, absolutely, he was wrong about our opening physical retail stores. The inventory implications alone would sink us. But he might be right about beginning our global push right away. We needed to rebrand ourselves as an emerging international computer corporation powerhouse, not some narrow, US-based mail-order PC-clone company.

It was September 1986. I had been with the company for four months, and we were still called PC's Limited. What a dreadful name. How in God's green earth could we ever build a brand around "PC's Limited," a name that mumbled "generic, undistinctive, common, meager, paltry, small, and narrow"?

The last time I wandered into this topic, wondering aloud about the branding implications of our corporate name, Michael was peeved. "You are disrespecting our name!" he said. "Lee, how can we move forward with our employees, customers, suppliers, when you, the president of our company, don't show respect for our name?"

It wasn't a matter of disrespect. I was beyond disrespect. I didn't have the courage to say what I was thinking: Our name stinks.

I began to suppose there probably would never be a perfect time to get going on our international operations. When is there ever a perfect time to get going on something you gotta get going on? While I'm prone to action, Michael Dell *is* action. We both embraced the attitude that, when faced with a choice, you pick something, and your actions—not the choice itself—will make it right. The thing that you'll regret is when you just sat there and stewed over the choice. But at that moment I was worried that our company didn't have enough money. And Michael was thinking, "Oh, for God's sake."

I had nothing against going international in theory. In fact, my college mentor Wayne Stark had instilled in me a love of travel. He was the person who had revealed to me the imagination-expanding importance of visiting countries not your own. Thanks to Wayne, in fact, I had taken one of my most adventurous trips, the summer after my first year at Harvard Business School.

Wayne and I stayed in touch after I graduated, which wasn't difficult since I was still on campus, pursuing a PhD in nuclear physics. But then I left A&M to enroll at Harvard. Wayne had been goading me by telephone all semester to go to Africa. There was a coal freighter leaving for Hamburg, Germany. If I could get down to Newport News, Virginia, he could get me a free trip across the Atlantic, arrange for someone to buy me a train ticket from Hamburg to Geneva, and get me an internship covering room and board there, where Esso Africa was centered. Then it was up to me to charm my way from Geneva to Africa. Esso was a wholly owned subsidiary of one of the largest oil companies in the world, formerly Standard Oil Company, branded as Esso in its thousands of gas stations, later to be renamed Exxon, today's Exxon Mobil. Esso was the phonetic pronunciation of its parent company, Standard Oil ("SO"), and once there, my job was to study its trade accounts receivable problem. One way to measure trade accounts receivable is if you ship somebody a product and a day later they haven't paid you, you now have an accounts receivable that is one day old. Esso Africa's trade accounts receivable for certain African countries were running as many as six months late. My job was to study other Esso accounts that were in good standing, in places like Switzerland and Cyprus, and to figure out how to implement their methods in Africa.

Aside from the sketchiness of my itinerary, there was also the problem of Cash Flo. Not the income stream, although that was always an issue. "Cash Flo" was the nickname students had for Florence Glynn, the infamous woman who was the registrar for Harvard Business School. A square-jawed, no-nonsense but kind-faced woman of about fifty, she knew every excuse, every ploy. After decades of watchful attention over incoming students, she parsed and sifted every story, always on the lookout for any wanna-be MBAs who might be lying about the money they needed.

At the start of my first semester, in September 1965, I found myself sitting across the desk from Cash Flo in her office at Morgan Hall. "Miss Glynn, I have no money," I told her. The expression on her face seemed to say, "It is not possible for anyone to show up at Harvard Business School without a plan of how to pay for it." She told me that the B School didn't give out scholarships.

"I am the oldest of six children," I explained. "My dad died over two years ago. Mother is an elementary school teacher, and she was left with a lot to carry. . . ."

Was Cash Flo wavering after hearing about my dad's death from cancer, my being the oldest of six kids, my mother's job teaching fifth-graders, and my having been completely on my own since high school, paying for all of my undergraduate and graduate studies through scholarships and work? Was she beginning to see that I had arrived fresh from the world of nuclear physics, with the financial ignorance that sometimes attaches to doodle-brained scientists without a lick of business sense?

I delivered my knockout punch: "Miss Glynn, I lost everything I owned on the way up here. I packed it all in a box and put it on a Greyhound bus—a Greyhound bus that lost my box somewhere along the way. My box, with everything I own, never made it."

Cash Flo's eyes narrowed. She asked me to give her the name and phone number of the person I spoke with at Greyhound. Someone had told me to never lie to Florence Glynn. Because if she found out—and she was a ferret finder-outer of lies—well, you just didn't want to go there.

No problem. Cash Flo would soon discover everything I said was true. My letter sweaters and jackets that would have helped protect me against the winter-freezing sleet off the Charles River, my slide rules, my books, all my clothes, even the Blessed Virgin Mary statue that I won because I knew the Baltimore catechism better than any of my fourth-grade classmates at St. Charles Borromeo—everything was gone. Somewhere between Texas and Cambridge, someone had taken my stuff.

Cash Flo's face softened. She told me that Harvard would help me get through my first year but I'd need a well-paying job the following summer so that I could pay for the rest of my time in graduate school.

Somehow, and with Cash Flo's help, I made it through that first year at Harvard. She also had made it very clear that I needed to make money the following summer to fund my second year. But Wayne Stark was convinced that an internship in Africa (unpaid, beyond room and board) was central to my development.

With school out, I hitchhiked down to Manhattan, sleeping overnight on a stranger's sofa while loud shouts and music played outside in an annual festival of the Little Italy community. From there, I thumbed some rides that got me to Newport News, Virginia, where I located the coal freighter owned by Stavros Niarchos, the Greek shipping magnate that Mr. Stark had found for me. After a couple of days and nights drinking with the Greek crew, we lifted anchor for the two-week voyage across the Atlantic.

Every evening was movie time. Unfortunately, there was only one movie. The tiny Greek crewmen and I watched *Lawrence of Arabia* every night for two weeks. To this day, any images of Peter O'Toole still evoke twinges of nausea because we had a particularly rough crossing, storm after storm. Arriving in Geneva, I moved into in a student *pensione* at Cite Universitaire.

My boss at Esso Africa liked me—not enough to give me any money above what I needed for food and my room, but enough to send me to Africa to see if I could gain some understanding of Esso's trade accounts receivable problem. After a summer of gallivanting around Africa, I submitted my insights on how to solve Esso's problem. The truth of the matter was that I didn't have many insights. Part of the report was simply reporting back what I had heard from Esso's various African subsidiaries. In the end, I wrote that the company's trade accounts receivable problem was inherently cultural in nature. The Esso customers saw nothing wrong with taking several months to pay their accounts because that's how their business culture worked. Forcing them to pay their accounts more quickly might lead to a longer time between payments or even not paying at all. I saw it as a deep cultural attitude that wasn't going to change.

Then it was September, and I was once again in Florence Glynn's Harvard office. She wasn't happy when I told her I had spent the summer in Africa as an unpaid intern.

I explained that I needed to learn about accounts receivable in foreign operations, so I had gone first to Cyprus where the taxi driver and I had to hit the floor when fighting broke out between the Turks and the Greeks. I then told her about tromping around the ruins of Carthage in Tunisia, about the Algerian soldiers kicking down the door of the room where I was staying in Algiers, about the souks of Morocco, and about the outbreak of a revolution in Nigeria.

At some point, Cash Flo threw up her hands. She had heard enough. She told me that I would spend the rest of that academic year getting up every morning and delivering newspapers to my classmates and other students living on campus. "Thank God, you're young and strong," she said. "You're not going to get much sleep this year."

—o—

It's 5:00 a.m. and time to get up.

I've got a bunch of newspapers to deliver. I've got to unpack and sort out big bundles of *New York Times* and *Wall Street Journal*s stacked next to Harvard Way, the narrow street that threads through Harvard Business School. In wintertime my papers are often buried under snow.

There are seven dormitories named after former US treasury secretaries: Hamilton, Chase, Mellon, McCulloch, Gallatin, Morris, and Glass. The halls are three stories high with steep stairwells, no problem running up, but I have to be careful coming down because the steps are too narrow for my size 18 feet.

Most of my classmates aren't up yet. They'll complain if their morning newspaper is late. My long legs take three steps at a time going up, four at a time going down. I'm getting skinnier by the day. I have no choice but to do this. I need the money to help pay for the high cost of going to Harvard.

Harvard has been hard for me. More than hard, impossible. The lack of sleep, my humiliating inability to speak up in class, my incompetence as a writer (all of my written analyses of cases have come back with a giant U for Unsatisfactory, what we called an F at Texas A&M). Perhaps even worse, I feel no kinship with the subject material. I feel I'm slipping more and more into exhaustion and discouragement.

The Harvard Business School classrooms were small amphitheaters seating 100 students, with the professor standing in the well. I sat in the back row, hoping to be invisible even at my height. And then Professor McNaughton looked my way.

"Mr. Walker, is there anything you'd like to contribute?"

"No, sir."

"Are you sure?"

I nodded my head.

"Mr. Walker, please see me in my office right after class."

Shortly after, there I sat, across from Professor John McNaughton in his office piled high with books and periodicals. He studied me for a few seconds before leaning forward on his desk.

"Mr. Walker, I'm not going to fail you."

I said nothing.

After a pause he said, "I don't believe in failing students who have a speech impediment."

I said nothing.

"Mr. Walker, you do have a speech impediment, don't you?"

I hunched over and lowered my eyes. "I'm not sure," I mumbled.

I got up, walked down the hall, then outside across the green fields that led down to the Charles River, climbed the stairs to my room in McCulloch Hall, and curled up in bed in utter defeat. It wasn't just that I was terrified of public speaking, which I was. I was beyond butterflies: snake-pit scared, psychotically frightened.

Why was this such a problem for me?

The gods of circumstance and chance had been cruel in bringing me, the poster child for introversion, to Harvard Business School, the citadel of capitalism and epicenter of extroversion, a place where speaking with glib certainty was the coin of the realm.

To succeed at the B School, you had to speak often. That was the rule of the game. Had I known the rule of the game, I wouldn't have gone there. And if I had known the amount of money they expected you to fork over, I certainly wouldn't have gone. None of this made any sense to me. For others maybe, but not me. So why had I gone to Harvard?

When I was working on my PhD in nuclear physics, it occurred to me that I should make a visit to NASA since the agency was paying all of my education expenses.

I went down on a Friday and met recently minted PhDs in physics who were now working there. And I had a chance to see what they were working on. Afterward, I went back to my hotel room thinking no way in hell am I going to work there. Working there would kill my imagination, I thought.

All those years . . . now what was I going to do?

The next day I went to the wedding of Lynn Merritt, a basketball teammate from Texas A&M. At the reception I sat across the table from a man named Dick Zartler. He had just graduated from a place called Harvard Business School and now had a job running a business for DuPont.

I didn't know what any of those words meant. But I wanted to know. So I asked Dick Zartler lots of questions. And at some point he said, "You really ought to apply to Harvard Business School."

When I got back to College Station, I wrote a letter to Harvard requesting the admission forms. It was the only place I applied. In retrospect, I should have done more research than just talking to someone at a wedding reception, a man I never saw again. But Wayne Stark encouraged me to apply, too. I knew that Wayne knew a Harvard Business School professor who had graduated from Texas A&M. He kept in touch with Aggie Larry Fouracre (Class of '47), who would eventually become dean of Harvard Business School. Wayne may have even made a call on my behalf, urging his fellow Aggie to put in a good word for me.

Then I got to Harvard, and the question was not whether to tough it out. The real question was whether I *could* tough it out. The Harvard Business School case method relied upon students bringing their life experiences to the party. Class discussions were the bone and marrow of the system there. Each student had to bring his knowledge of the world to the cut and thrust of back-and-forth arguments. I listened awestruck by the facile way in which others spoke about the worlds they came from, about the frameworks they had learned before going there.

I knew all about Schrödinger's Equation and about the exquisite beauty of the rapid convergence of certain infinite series. I was especially fond of the one that summed up to the wondrously irrational constant called "e," whose mysterious logarithms were at the core of the slide rule, the personal computer of that era. Somehow these mind frames I cherished never seemed relevant to the flow of our class discussions. Finally came my southern accent, the cherry on top of the whipped cream of business ignorance surrounding the vanilla ice cream of debilitating shyness.

In 1965 on the evening of November 9 around 5:30 I realized I couldn't go on. It was already dark outside when I walked into my room, C-43 in Chase Hall, sat on my bed, and accepted that it was time for me to quit. My two roommates, Leo and Chumporn, were away. It wouldn't take long to pack my one bag and leave a note so they would know they didn't have to drag the Charles River for my body. I'd cross over the river one last time, walk down to Harvard Square, catch the MTA downtown to the Boston bus station.

I put my one suitcase on the bed. I put in two pairs of socks. The lights went out. Chase C-43 was black. I waited for the light to come back on. And waited some more. I looked out the window and couldn't see any light anywhere. I put my suitcase on the floor and lay down to wait it out.

When I awoke, I could tell night had passed. I was groggy with sleep. I slept some more. Later when I awoke, it was lunchtime. I wasn't hungry, so I went back to bed and slept until suppertime. I walked over to Kresge, the building where we took our meals. One of my classmates asked me if I had prepared tomorrow's case analysis. When I said I had not, he told me that all the classes had been canceled because of a giant blackout that covered a million square miles. It was a historic power outage that had disrupted the lives of 80 million people.

I guessed that I must have slept almost twenty-four hours since the blackout began. I looked around. No one seemed to know that I had given up, quit. As I ate my dinner, I thought about how if the blackout had occurred a day later, I would have been halfway home to Texas. But it happened just after I put my socks in my suitcase, just before I wrote a note to my roommates.

The twenty-four hours of sleep had not erased my discouragement, but it had given me a provisional reprieve from my plan to flee this place. The core problems remained. I still couldn't find a way to participate in class discussions, I still was terminally shy, still couldn't relate to courses with soul-killing names like Managerial Economics, Reporting and Control, or the mind-numbing Human Behavior in Organizations. My twenty-four-hour sleep had not given me any capacity to absorb the marketing skills Professor Walter Salmon was trying to impart or savor the business policy questions Professor John Glover was attempting to convey. But the twenty-four-hour stay of execution had broken the momentum of the despair that had gripped me. I now felt like I had at least one more day of effort left in me to try to slog through this mess of a mistake I had made.

—◇—

Decades later, when the subject of international expansion came up with Michael Dell, I remembered the price I paid back at Harvard. In 1986 I didn't know if I had the smarts or stamina to begin setting up foreign operations on top of being president and chief financial officer. And even if I could muster the smarts and stamina, how much more could we stretch the rubber balloon of our balance sheet before it popped?

One thing was for sure. If we did expand to England, I'd have to find a crackerjack personality to start the operation there and run it. Someone who would be willing to set up an operation in a small corner of England somewhere, not a separate building, not a separate floor, not even a separate room, but a corner of somebody else's room with minimal overhead. We needed to find someone who could and would operate under the tight cash flow discipline that was our mantra. And someone who was a damn fine entrepreneur.

Aside from the international question, we had tons of other issues that spurred Michael's and my two-man walkabouts around the table. The PC industry had already started its brutal shakeout as Darwin's rule of the survival of the most adaptable had begun working its inexorable, grinding squeeze.

IBM, Apple, and Compaq had 50 percent market share. It took no particular prescience to see that our industry, like every boom industry that had ever been, would one day be dominated by a small handful of companies. How could little bitty PC's Limited be one of those winners?

The retail store puzzle tormented me. The argument for working through dealers by selling PC's Limited computers in their stores was seductive. At that time, people did not buy big-ticket items through the mail. If customers had to choose between buying something they could touch and see in a store versus buying from a company over the phone, a so-called mail-order firm, wouldn't those prospective customers usually buy from a store?

I was invited to Texas A&M to participate in a debate on this topic. Wayne Stark had officially retired from A&M around this time, but he was still a familiar presence in the Memorial Student Center. He wanted A&M to be a place of intellectual foment, a dueling ground for ideas, so he organized a debate about the future of the computer industry. He invited me to represent PC's Limited against McKinsey and Company, a well-known management consulting firm. During the debate, I took the position that in the fullness of time computers would become less of a novelty. Customers would be at least as likely to choose a firm like ours as one with a retail presence if for no other reason than we offered lower prices.

Two men from McKinsey and Company took the opposite argument. They believed that there was but little upside for a mail-order firm's growth potential. "Would you ever buy a car without sitting behind the steering wheel, without running your fingertips over the interior upholstery made of fine Corinthian leather?" they asked.

At the end of the debate, a vote was taken to determine who won. Ninety percent of the audience agreed with the McKinsey men. Before the debate, most of the Aggies in the audience were split 50/50 on the question. I suppose it helped that I was an Aggie (Class of '63) and the McKinsey guys sounded like they were from New Jersey. But my Aggieness wasn't enough. My debating skills moved the needle forty points—in the wrong direction.

It occurred to me driving home from Aggieland that there was probably no such thing as Corinthian leather. The power of McKinsey's dueling slide show technique with two projectors throwing up facts and figures was devastating. All I had was my opinions and tallness. Had I been a young, impressionable Aggie, I might have voted for McKinsey as well.

I was careful never to mention this story to Michael. He was fierce enough in his opinion without my revealing that McKinsey and Company and a whole room full of Aggies believed that to be big enough to survive and thrive, you had to sell through retail storefronts.

But for the life of me I could not accept that. I would not accept that.

—◦—

Michael and I continued to circle our table, playing catch and throw. I thank the Almighty to this day that it was a balloon and not a basketball. One of Michael's bullet passes would surely have cost me an eye or at least a dislocated finger.

An old teaching of Wayne Stark's would edge into my

mind from time to time. Mr. Stark had said that "the path to greatness is through service." Service. A neat word I liked a lot. It connoted a helping hand, kind-hearted assistance.

Hadn't I once been an altar boy who "served" mass every morning? Hadn't my dad stayed up nights filling and stacking sandbags in service to his community when the Missouri River threatened Kansas City back when I was ten years old living on Shady Lane across the street from St. Charles Borromeo Church? Wasn't service fundamental to the core teachings that had permeated my early Catholic training?

All that aside, the commercial implications of the word "service" were clear. In the increasingly concentrated world of personal computer companies, the winners would be the ones that took the best care of their customers, those companies that best served and supported their customers, those companies with the best service and support.

Service and support was a problem for us.

Again and again as we listened on the phone to our customers, the message came through loud and clear from large companies like General Motors, General Electric, general anything. They weren't buying from us because we had no service and support in the field. They could call us for help, they could send their computer back to us for repairs, but that was it. We were centered in Austin and had no presence beyond Austin. We were a mail-order firm.

We were in a bind. We didn't have the resources to create a field operation, yet we couldn't move forward without one. We couldn't raise money if we were strictly a mail-order firm, but we couldn't break away from being a mail-order firm if we couldn't raise money.

To Michael's credit, he never said, "Okay, 'Mr. Guru' Lee, what's the answer?" He knew I didn't have a clue what the answer was. And to my credit, I never said, "Well, you're the 'Boy Wonder' genius, you tell me the answer."

We just kept circling the table, pitching the world back and forth: Michael, confident we'd figure it out, and me, hoping we'd figure it out while fretting about how much money I could sign checks for on that particular day.

CHAPTER 8

The Retreat in Santa Rosa

"Fast enough to burn the sand off a desert floor."

Michael held the headline close so my nearsighted eyes could see the story. Dell had defeated IBM, Compaq, and everybody else in a head-to-head competition running a wide variety of power tests. *PC Magazine* had wanted to find out who had the fastest 386-model computer. The answer? Dell Computer.

That's right. Not only did we have the fastest computer, but we were now calling ourselves Dell Computer Corporation. We had finally changed our name from PC's Limited, just as we were starting to expand globally. I, for one, was relieved.

The glow on Michael's face was incandescent. His high-pitched giggle filled my office. I rubbed my right shoulder with my left hand, still recovering from being knocked back a few feet by the force of his high five when he burst into my office with the news. I had never seen him more excited. This was a big deal—a very big deal.

Michael tore out of my office, brandishing his June 1988 copy of *PC Magazine*. "Jay has got to see this." I could hear Michael charging down the hallway looking for Jay Bell, our technology whiz who had figured out how to make our machines faster than anyone else's.

"Burn the sand off a desert floor." My mind's eye jumped to an image of the parallel tire tracks of fire in the hit movie *Back to the Future*. The Michael in that 1985 movie, Michael

J. Fox as Marty McFly, time-travels in a souped-up DeLorean car that leaves a flaming trail behind as Libyan terrorists try to shoot him with a bazooka, only to see him vanish into a different time dimension. Doc Brown, his older coconspirator friend, called him "Future Boy." Well, our future boy was burning rubber, scorching the desert, according to *PC Magazine.*

The truth was, speed had always been one of our strengths. Back in 1986, when we were still PC's Limited, *PC Magazine* had called our 286 model "one of the first real potential 'IBM killers' . . . astoundingly fast." But the subtext of our real-world reality was that we still were missing some key parts before we could make the huge jump we needed to get away from the unfriendly fire of our competition, to move into another dimension.

Despite his exuberance about the speed of our machines, Michael knew we couldn't transform the company into a great company until we solved our service and support limitations. He knew we couldn't achieve greatness until large corporations believed we were more than a mail-order company and started buying from us.

Big corporate buyers didn't believe we were more than a mail-order company because we *were* a mail-order company. We had no presence outside of our home base in Austin. We didn't have enough money to create a service and support system that big companies demanded as a prerequisite for doing business with us. We couldn't raise the money we needed in the amounts we needed because we couldn't show potential investors we could sell our products to big corporations like GE and General Motors.

We were caught, surrounded in this space and time. We needed to invent our way out of this dimension we were in.

The Russian River flowed nearby on its way to the Pacific Ocean. On Friday afternoon, September 26, 1986, we arrived at the Vintner Inn in Santa Rosa, California, for a three-day think at what we hoped would be our breakout innovation place. Why the Vintner Inn? Why the Russian River Valley? I don't remember.

But I do remember that if we were going to discover a path to a different dimension, to be more than a mail-order company, we needed to find a quiet, generative place that would help us shatter our normal mind habits. A place where we could spark the inspiration we needed to match our aspirations. We didn't have the possibility of greatness without some imagination breakthrough.

There were ten of us and a facilitator. Six of us were full-time employees, four were outside consultants or friends. As an icebreaker, our facilitator began our Friday-evening session with a description of one of the great gizmos of all time, the Thermos. He told us the story of its incremental chance-driven history, its invention by James Dewar, and its appropriation by others who called it the Thermos. The Thermos, a cool contraption for keeping your hot cocoa hot or your iced tea cold, leading to one of the oldest clichéd jokes: How does it know?

Our facilitator followed his Thermos history lesson by asking us, "What makes you happy?"

I don't recall my answer. It was probably something like, cherry pie, just like Grandma Baker used to make. Nor do I recollect anyone else's answer—except for Jim Seymour's. Seymour, the person who first introduced me to Michael. What made him happy? Fly-fishing made Seymour happy. Now what could be more minuscule than a fly in the immense paws of the 400-pound Seymour as he impaled an imaginary bug on an invisible hook, his surprisingly supple fingers threading a tiny wisp of fly life on his fishing line as he performed in large-gestured pantomime.

I recalled a few years before when Seymour dragged me to the Colorado River for my one and only fly-fishing outing. He waddled to midstream, his massive chest covered by a tan, multipocketed jacket containing an astonishing number of teeny doodads. I caught nothing. Neither did he. Fly-fishing had not made me happy, but somehow it made Seymour happy.

After the happy question came wishing time when we were asked to make our wishes known around this service and support question. I don't remember much about the wishes that were made, with one exception.

One reason I remember that singular wish was because it was so mindless, so impractical, so lacking in any appreciation for our money constraints. I could only groan inwardly. It was against the rules to voice or show any criticism of anyone's wishes. Only with great discipline did I stifle my annoyance—and embarrassment, because it was my fault. I had taken a chance and invited a twenty-one-year-old salesperson, Kim Roell, to be part of our ten-person team. Kim was the antiparticle to Seymour's vastness—and easily the youngest among us, except for Future Boy, of course.

She said, "I wish I could tell my customers we would fix their problems right away. We would have a technician on their doorstep the next day."

I bit my lower lip. I chided myself, thinking that next time I needed to take more time and care when deciding who gets invited to a crucial meeting. A technician. On their doorstep. The next day.

But that wasn't all. Kim topped her wish with a cherry: "And I wish it were free."

Free. So simple-minded and naïve. I could scarcely keep from wagging my whole body into a huge "no, no, no." I thought, "You cannot ignore gravity, and you cannot repeal fundamental economics. We cannot afford this waste of time."

The moment passed quickly as other wishes were offered and written on big pieces of butcher paper that were then taped up to hang around our meeting room. Part of me felt a slight growing desperation. Nothing transformative seemed to be happening. God forbid if we had traveled almost 2,000 miles, spending many multiples of our capital base, only to limp home with the news that we had no news.

—◦—

Five months passed. In February 1987, at Logan Airport in Boston, Massachusetts, I was running to catch an American Airlines flight to London. Kelly Guest was trotting beside me. We'd just finished a marathon two-day negotiation with Honeywell Bull. I was rumpled and unshaven, my loose tie flapping. How the hell did Kelly always manage to look like he just stepped off a *GQ* magazine cover, perfectly attired, every hair in place?

Kelly was one key to Dell's secret sauce of success. So much more than an attorney, he was our number one negotiator. I thought I was a damn fine negotiator until I saw Kelly in action. Compared with him, I was a capable but amiable donkey.

We had wrapped up our negotiations with Honeywell Bull, makers of mainframes and now PCs themselves, an hour and a half earlier. I signed on the dotted line before our mad dash to the airport. For every computer we shipped out our door, our deal memo said, we'd pay Honeywell Bull just over thirty bucks. In exchange, their field support technicians—the critical resource we did not have—would fix any computer of ours for up to one full year after we shipped it. A clean, simple deal. Voilà! We had on-site service and support through Honeywell's national service network. And they had a profitable cash flow stream—a win-win for both of us.

And we didn't pass the $30 cost on to our customers.

My thinking was this: If I took the point of view that we had just added $30 of cost to each computer, then my engineering/accounting brain argued for increasing our prices by at least $30 plus some markup. But I went to my nonlinear quantum physics brain, which began to hypothesize that if we said our service was free, the message our customers would hear would be our complete confidence in our computers. I thought our sales might grow exponentially and our fixed overhead for every computer would go down at a much greater rate than the $30. In other words, even if our sales doubled, our general and administrative overhead would not because it wouldn't require us to add another president or anything like that. While this had elements of voodoo economics, I thought it was worth a try. I decided to go with the complete aspiration Kim Roell had wished for in the Russian River Valley.

All of this was possible, thanks to our manufacturing system, courtesy of Tandem's Bob Swem. We knew precisely the individual details about each component in each computer we shipped. Each PC was bar-coded and had its own identity. We could tell the Honeywell Bull service guy exactly what parts he should take when making his service call. IBM and Compaq could not match this because they mass-produced "unpersonalized" personal computers. The whole notion of particularizing individual units was mind-blowing at that time. In our case, constraint had bred imagination. We turned our inefficiency into a breakthrough. Had we had the money to fix our manufacturing issues, I don't know if we would have come up with such a creative solution. For us, it was very personal. We had the systems to walk our talk. The other guys didn't.

Now Kelly and I were off to England to try to get something going there. I had changed my mind about our international presence. Michael had the better argument. If we were going to convince the world that we were a global player, then we had to get started on being a global player. Even if that meant we only occupied an inexpensive corner of a room in some dusty back alley on the outskirts of London. So I switched my vote in a board of directors meeting. The motion passed unanimously by a 2-0 vote. In triumph, a smiling Michael made a pretty hook shot of our balloon ball globe into an imaginary basketball hoop I made with a circle of my two arms.

—○—

Such a silly wish made that day along the Russian River. A technician on the customer's doorstep the next day. For free. Sweet, naïve Kim's idea was not so dumb after all. We all finally realized that at the end of our three-day think. Her wish was the bolt of lightning needed to power up our flux capacitor, the necessary service and support end-component to our Swem manufacturing system.

Kelly and I settled into our plane seats and fastened our seat buckles with two minutes to spare before takeoff across the Atlantic. We were both punch-drunk from the exhaustion of hammering out the Honeywell deal. While neither of us could grasp all the implications of the previous five months of imagination in action, we both had some sense of what a game changer this would be in our company's history.

We were now ready to launch our company into another dimension, leaving flaming tire tracks behind.

CHAPTER 9

The Crash

It sounded like the end of the world.

I pulled over, keeping my car engine running, and listened to the latest news on the radio. It was October 19, 1987, and the stock market had lost a quarter of its value, twice as bad as Black Friday in 1929. Twenty-three percent of market value gone, vanished, evaporated in one day.

What rotten bad luck. We were a week away from closing Dell's very first stock sale. If we just could have gotten our money before the worst money day there ever was. Now it seemed impossible. When the last giant market crash happened sixty years earlier, it began the Great Depression. That catastrophic day was only half as bad as this one.

My mind began to conjure up future soup lines stretching across Austin, brand new Hoovervilles, shanty towns springing up and down the city's central creeks. Would they be called Ronnietowns? Or Reaganvilles? Was this market implosion triggered by the crap and corruption on Wall Street we had been reading about? Ivan Boesky and Mike Milken and his Drexel Lambert den of thieves, for example?

I recalled two federal agents who had said that cocaine was used or accepted by 90 percent of the people on Wall Street. That had seemed like sensational overstatement until now. Had coke-stoked hallucinations built a drug-fueled bubble before it popped?

Was this the giant tsunami the gold bugs had been predicting? I thought back to when I was a silver bug, loading up on silver before giving up on precious metals in 1978. My timing had been off, in this case by several thousand days.

I trudged up the thirteen steps in front of our Headway Circle headquarters. Michael needed to know the bad news right away. He was standing over his desk. Littered with computer parts, it looked more like the workbench of a mad scientist than the desk of an executive. He looked up as I dragged in.

I told Michael that our financing deal had just died, that market traders must be jumping off window ledges and the gutters of Wall Street had to be running with their blood.

Had I known the market would drop another 7 percent the following Monday, when we were scheduled to close the stock sale, I might have skipped meeting with Michael and headed straight for the nearest bar.

But there we were. And Michael was making a mess doing something that always put a glow on his face, pulling apart some competitor's computer, bit by bit, poring over its inner design, its bill of materials, its technical details. His desk looked like the table of an obsessed teenager, which, come to think of it, it almost was.

"Hmmmm, too bad," he said after I shared my apocalyptic news. He turned back to his mini demolition derby, humming something unrecognizable.

We were definitely the odd couple: me, the anxiety-ridden forty-six-year-old; he, the twenty-something who seemed impervious to the fears that plague many of the rest of us.

It was as if I had just told him that Chez Zee, one of my favorite Austin restaurants, had discontinued its beloved coconut cream pie. How regrettable, unfathomable, but you know dessert fads. They come and they go.

Michael squinched his nose, grabbed a screwdriver, and started a fresh assault on the motherboard on his desk. It was a microcosmic moment in our relationship, which had deepened over the past year and a half since I told him I had changed my mind and would help him as best I could. Little had I imagined how much we would get done and how quickly we would get it done.

Now to miss getting the money we needed so badly by only a week and a day. We were selling more than $150 million a year, five times what the sales rate had been eighteen months earlier. But our balance sheet showed invested capital of only $1,000. We couldn't continue with this small amount of money supporting our operations.

Our manufacturing quality, great service and support, fledgling international operations, direct sales model, and product technology were all combining to give us accelerating traction in the marketplace. But we hadn't accelerated quite far enough, fast enough. We needed more operating capital. Maybe if we'd been a little larger, a little further along, a bit more profitable with more of a track record.

I suspected we had precious little time and guessed we had to move quickly. While we hadn't foreseen the details of the market debacle that was looming in 1987, we had been smart enough to know that it was time to find the best possible Wall Street investment banker. Neither Michael nor I had any idea of who that should be. We only knew the two of us needed to cruise around New York City until we figured it out.

Earlier that year, in the spring of 1987, I had made a booking for us to stay at the Plaza Hotel on Fifty-ninth Street and Fifth Avenue. I loved the funky, faded-past feeling there and the dining room. Michael hated my choice. It was an old-fashioned place not remotely wired for the connectivity Michael wanted.

Once there, he gave me a look that said he was willing to put up with my out-of-date fuddy-duddiness, but only out of affection. Next time, couldn't we stay at some place with a little more with-it-ness?

Where else could we get better eggs Benedict with extra Benedict on them? Where else could we have such immediate access to the toys across the street at FAO Schwarz? Where else could we have such immediate access to Central Park and its zoo?

E. F. Hutton had invited us to visit. The company was aggressive in its outreach to companies looking for capital, and we must have looked interesting enough to its representatives because they made a strong pitch for our business. The company's advertising jingle was pervasive. When E. F. Hutton talks, people listen. Except the place spoke lethargic inertness to us. We didn't feel the energy we were looking for. We learned much later that E. F. Hutton was in a financial crisis of its own and was only months away from a shotgun marriage to Shearson Lehman American Express. At the time of our visit, the E. F. Hutton walls and halls must have talked silently to us. Thank God, we listened.

We then visited Paine Webber in its new headquarters in midtown Manhattan on Avenue of the Americas. Though Michael's mother worked as a stockbroker for Paine Webber in Houston, after exploring the New York headquarters, neither Michael nor I felt a fit with what we heard and saw. We shared a feeling that Paine Webber felt low-energy.

But when we walked into Goldman Sachs, there was almost an instant click. The place pulsated with the kind of energy, dynamism, and smartness we were searching for. The people we met there came across as super-competent and high-energy. Goldman wanted our business and pitched us hard on why the company was right for us. Michael and I knew we had found our Wall Street partner and investment banker.

In the months that followed, Goldman reps worked with us to get our investor pitch created and refined. They praised us for what we had accomplished and said we had everything in place we needed for a successful offering. There were only two things we needed to fix, but they were relatively easy. We listened as Goldman told us that I could no longer serve as both president and chief financial officer. We had to hire someone else to be our CFO and who would report to me.

The truth was, I was exhausted from filling both roles. It had been necessary, I thought, to keep pretty much absolute control over the money since I had watched so many high-fliers spin out of control when they lost control of their finances, lost control of their balance sheet. I had kept total control by signing all the checks, never allowing more money to go out than came in.

Goldman's second recommendation was that we needed to add two people to our board of directors. Michael and I were not enough; the minimum number required was at least four.

When we asked if they had anyone in mind, they named George Kozmetsky and Bobby Ray Inman because both had great reputations that would dress up our board nicely. Kozmetsky was the former dean of the University of Texas Business School and a respected entrepreneur and philanthropist. Inman, a retired US admiral, had been the director of the National Security Agency and had recently become the chairman of the Federal Reserve Bank of Dallas.

That was it. Our business model was spot-on. Our performance in the market was gaining momentum. We only needed cosmetic surgery to improve our appearance.

Michael and I could barely contain our excitement, but this was not the time to show any immaturity by screaming and high-fiving. I repeated what they had said, that all we needed to do was hire a CFO and add two members to our board of directors. Do those two things, they told us, and they would help us raise $30 million, a crucial and welcome addition to our paid-in capital base. At this point our annual sales were running at about $150 million, giving us absolutely no margin of error, no buffer against unforeseen difficulties or any screw-ups on our part.

We soon accomplished both things requested by Goldman Sachs, completed our stock offering prospectus, and began touring the country in early 1987 doing the prerequisite "road show" when we were able to take breaks from the day-to-day business operations. A "road show" is the first step before going public, in which a company goes out first to its investment firm's Rolodex of contacts. From the point of view of our Goldman Sachs advisors, if we had a good story and they put us in front of 10,000 people from their Rolodex, 100 of them might say yes. We had a short presentation that they wanted us to give to every potential investor. Talk about a lack of creativity. I kept wanting to change the presentation each time to make the experience less boring. I would frequently stray off script, but they just wanted us to hammer the same points over and over again.

But we were nearly derailed by another potential crisis. IBM, the mighty IBM, finally delivered the knockout blow that my friend Ron Carroll had predicted when he and I took our Cat Mountain walk together the year before.

"Dear Dell Computer Corporation: We have reason to believe you may be infringing some of our patents."

Well, no kidding!

IBM's letter went on: "Please contact us as soon as possible to discuss this matter."

Soon after receiving the IBM letter, Michael and I flew into LaGuardia Airport in Queens, rented a car, and drove to Purchase, New York, IBM's intellectual property headquarters, maybe an hour's drive north of New York City. We stayed overnight in a nearby hotel. At breakfast the next morning, *USA Today* blared a front-page story that Dell Computer was about to have its first-ever stock sale.

What great timing. Emmett Murtha, the man we were about to meet at IBM, must have seen this article. IBM had a gajillion patents. We had exactly zero patents. We were going into a life-or-death meeting with an IBM man who had a nuclear cannon. We had a water pistol with no water—zero in it.

As we pulled onto the drive that led up to the IBM building, I gaped at the landscaped grounds. The place reminded me of the Emerald City in *The Wizard of Oz*. There were acres and acres of freshly mown grass as we drove up the winding drive-way, all trimmed perfectly along the edges. On and on it went, an epic driveway to remember.

Then it came to me. With this level of overhead, maybe IBM was vulnerable. Maybe I had it backward. Maybe they, not us, were the ones in trouble, at least in personal computers, com-peting against aggressive upstarts like us without a blade of grass in our cost structure. Behind their Oz-like curtain, was it possible, even with all those cords and levers they were pulling, that they were ultimately powerless in the low-cost, down-and-dirty, hardscrabble world of personal computers?

As Michael and I arrived at the charming, almost friend-ly-looking structure at the end of the long driveway, we entered and soon were offered hot tea served in exquisite china by our host. I thought, sip, don't slurp, and for heaven's sake, don't spill on the Persian rug. Michael was quiet, declining to drink anything.

Emmett Murtha, director of licensing for IBM, was friendly and professional, and he tried to put us at ease with amiable small talk. I guessed he was in his late forties, a few years older than me.

Finally, he got down to business. He said his purpose was not to destroy us, merely to have us pay some small amount of money for every computer we shipped since we were benefit-ing from the use of IBM technology, which we were obviously using. He wanted all of our competitors to pay the same rate because they were infringing as well. He wanted a level playing field. Who could argue against a level playing field?

I asked what this level playing field would cost us. He replied that 3 percent of sales was IBM's price for a full licensing agreement. Michael and I shot a glance at each other. By now, we could almost read each other's minds. We could live with this. The arrangement would give us precious time to grow strong, and in time, someday, maybe we would have our own patents. Maybe future negotiations might be more balanced. Maybe in time we could reduce that 3 percent. Maybe even make that 3 percent go away.

I asked Mr. Murtha to write up something for our attorney to study and told him that I thought what he had outlined would allow us to do business together. IBM could have put us out of business that morning but chose not to do so. We were free to move forward. Our latest challenge was solved.

I also thought that IBM had committed a colossal blunder. What I didn't anticipate was the degree of the blunder, one that would one day help drive IBM out of the PC business entirely.

—◆—

On October 26, a week after the 1987 market crash, I could barely go through the motions of making it through the day. I wondered if I needed to attend some kind of refresher leadership retreat to learn how to be resilient, strong, and inspiring, particularly on those days when I didn't want to get out of bed.

I told everyone I was having a massive allergy attack to explain my red, watery eyes and runny nose that day. My sopping handkerchief was not a very pleasant or effective mask to cover my weepy hangdog face. Later in the day, Michael's assistant, Kay Banda, came rushing in. Goldman Sachs was on the phone, but Michael was nowhere to be found.

I took the call and asked what was going on just as Michael walked in the door. The Goldman Sachs team began by describing how nasty the market drop was, calling it a complete catastrophe. Michael and I looked at each other. They described how deals scheduled for that day were postponed indefinitely, that most had died. We nodded silently. Then they told us that one deal had gone through, pausing for dramatic effect.

"Yours!" they screamed.

Michael beamed and then knocked me halfway across the room with the force of his high five. I plopped down on the floor in sheer disbelief.

They explained that our offering had been so strong that there had been an oversubscription of investors who wanted in. While that number had dropped dramatically after the market crash, in the end there were enough who still believed in Dell to get us our $30 million.

Michael and I looked at each other. Coconut cream pie was back on the Chez Zee menu.

—◦—

At Dell, and with Goldman Sachs's help, we had sold the market on our concept of the direct model. It wasn't a new idea, but as Michael writes in *Direct from Dell*, the way we approached direct selling is what set us apart. Not only did we sell direct, but we also designed and developed our own products rather than selling someone else's. We manufactured our own products rather than reselling someone else's. We serviced and supported our own products. In short, we were a fully integrated computer company that happened to sell direct to our customers rather than relying on stores or some other intermediary. That's why our deal had survived in the midst of the 1987 market crash.

If you think about it, everything you do in life involves sales. Whether you're selling yourself or your preference for which movie you and your date are going to see, you're trying to persuade someone to buy your point of view.

When I mention sales to my students, their first response is often "yuck." The word has such a Willy Loman–esque quality. Even after the concept made a thirty-two-year-old Michael Dell the richest man in Texas, articles would still refer to the business model of direct sales to customers as "déclassé." But I believe it is such a central idea, such an important skill to master. I lucked into learning about sales because one of my earliest mentors felt so strongly he wept over it. In the end, this idea helped give me a personal breakout strategy.

Once upon a time I worked with a man named Bill Spicer, a marketing executive at Esso Africa. It was that summer I spent interning at Esso Africa between semesters at Harvard Business School. I remember how Bill took me out for dinner in Geneva. He was triumphant. He had just speculated in Burndy stock (I hadn't known what that meant until he told me), and he had made a small killing. I didn't know you could make money that fast.

He asked me to guess what he was going to do with his stock profit. I had no idea. He quickly told me that he was going to buy a red Porsche. When he took possession of his new car on my last day in Geneva, he invited me along to see what his new baby could do on the road.

We headed east, faster and faster. I watched the light poles flash by until they seemed a blur. When the speedometer went past 200, I closed my eyes.

Death deferred, we arrived at a little restaurant on Lake Geneva for cold white wine and elegant flounder meunière. I had never known my taste buds could soar to heaven and linger.

Bill Spicer got drunk. Bill Spicer started crying. In between tears he begged me not to make the mistake he had made. Then he started blubbering.

Through sobs, he told of his Stanford MBA. How he started high up in Esso but now at forty was stalled in his career.

Because he hadn't paid his dues, hadn't sold stuff, hadn't worked in the field. Now he was stuck. He was forty and miserable. He asked me to promise that I wouldn't start at the top. He wanted me to start at the bottom, selling stuff.

I wondered if should base my life on a promise to a drunk man.

Bill Spicer kept insisting, getting more tearful and determined to intervene in my life and save me. To put him out of his misery, I said I would follow his advice.

During my last semester at Harvard Business School, after another defeated, deflating day in class, I opened my mail to find an invitation to come down to New York City to meet with the executives of the Cryogenic Department of Union Carbide, an international conglomerate and industry leader in chemicals and plastics. A big company—Fortune 500 big. But I didn't feel like I was a big-company guy. I couldn't put it into words at the time. Years later, a colleague named George Simpson affirmed what I felt when he said he thought I was more of an entrepreneur. I didn't even know what the term meant then. But slowly, over five years or so, incidents of people saying things like that, spending my first year working for a large company, then being thrown into the entrepreneurial pit at a small subsidiary company, then going back to a larger corporation, I began to understand the initial feeling I had had, the sense that I wouldn't thrive in the rough-and-tumble of such a big environment.

But I didn't have that insight at the time Union Carbide came calling during my last semester at Harvard. While the word "cryogenics" may conjure images of corpses perfectly preserved for some date-uncertain resurrection on earth, an appealing idea for a former altar boy like me, many industries rely on liquid nitrogen, oxygen, and other gases for more everyday jobs than daring to defy death.

Union Carbide liked my résumé—the physics thing, the

basketball thing, the overseas experience thing—and thought I might fit in, making $12,000 a year (the lowest offer made to me) and spending half my time in the field selling.

Ghosts of Bill Spicer appeared in my head. Half of my time in the field selling, and the other half of my job assisting the assistant of the smallest department in all of Union Carbide, one that made and sold cryogenic equipment.

Maybe this wouldn't feel like working for a giant company if I pretended the Cryogenic Department was an itty-bitty company that just happened to be on the eighth floor of the skyscraper at 270 Park Avenue in midtown Manhattan, the busiest single commercial district in the United States, and that just happened to have a giant neighbor in the same building with the same owner.

I met the man who would be my boss. Al Flamm looked Phoenician. He had huge, expressive eyes. And he sounded like Socrates. All he did was ask questions, great questions, questions that were connected to what had just been said.

I wondered if that was how he conducted himself in business, by never uttering a declarative sentence. (Turned out, that was exactly what he did. This cryogenic Socrates had figured out how to dominate by interrogation.)

By then I had reached my defining decision criteria. I wanted to work for a person who would be willing to teach me, mentor me, and take a genuine interest while helping me design my future life. And, taking Bill Spicer's advice, I decided I should learn how to sell.

I said yes to Union Carbide and the Cryogenic Department job. I wouldn't be making nearly as much money as in the other offers I received, but I would be able to pay off my Harvard debt in five years. Maybe I wasn't maximizing my money, but I was above the necessary threshold.

I felt that I was selling out in a sense by joining a big

company, but I didn't invent the world, didn't invent gravity, didn't invent those invisible mathematical constants that govern everything.

With as much glad grace as I could muster, I was surrendering to the multiple realities of money, debt, and adulthood. All that drivel about doing what you love, pursuing your passion? You do what you gotta do. And then hope you can learn to love it.

A year went by with Carbide. I sold some stuff. I wasn't a great salesman, but I wasn't terrible. My main problem was I seemed to always be getting lost and not finding where my customers were. (This was in the days before GPS.)

My very first day driving out of Manhattan, I was supposed to go to a welding shop in East Haven, Connecticut. I got there about two hours after I had planned to arrive. I hadn't told the welding shop owner I was coming, thinking it was better just to lurch in and sweep him off his feet.

I walked in at about 5:00 p.m., ducking through the low door. The owner was on the phone and about to make a call. He asked who I was, and then he told me that he was just about to call our competitor to place an order for 300 acetylene cylinders. When he asked what our price would be, I fumbled for the price list. He said yes without negotiating, thank goodness, for if he had pushed me at all, I would have been lost.

I immediately called back to Union Carbide's offices, triumphant on my first day on the road attempting to sell something to somebody.

It was a good first year. I came to understand that empathy was key. Listening, trying to understand as much as possible the full context of my customers' lives. It wasn't just about facts and figures and sales price; it was also about their feelings and identity. It was about trying to help them solve whatever problem was at hand, and it was about connecting with them even if in that moment they couldn't or wouldn't buy from me. I liked it when they seemed glad to see me, if for no other reason than to tease me about my outlandish size, or my being from Texas, or an Aggie, or of Polish descent. This interpersonal, seemingly silly stuff was only a lubricant for the fundamental engine of whether I could save them money, or make their operation more efficient, or help them solve some problem. This selling thing was a revelation to me. Since I may have been ever so subtly tinged with physics brain—an internal world that encourages the avoidance of any external emotional stimuli—these empathic opportunities were a constant source of surprise and wonder. After I received an order, no matter how small, I would sit in my car in the parking lot outside, suffused with a joy completely disproportionate to the size of the transaction. I was filled with a sense that the trust I had placed in this strange counterintuitive activity called sales was being paid back to me in copious psychic income.

When I wasn't trying to sell something to someone, I was trailing alongside my Socratic boss, watching him perform brilliant feats of verbal jujitsu over and over again. I sponged up his technique, thinking that one day with him was worth two years at Harvard Business School. To be fair, without the Harvard label on my forehead, I wouldn't have gotten the chance to study my Socrates, to immerse myself in his techniques of running a business.

Was I a good salesperson? I don't think so. But I was determined and authentic, and I knew the product. In any enterprise, where does that business start? Somebody has to sell something to someone else. The problem with a lot of us guys from Harvard, Stanford, or any other upper-crust school is often that we want to start our business careers by talking about enterprise models and mergers and acquisitions. Selling 300 tanks of acetylene gas? I don't think so. But someone like Bill Spicer would say, "That's where it starts. It's fundamental." For me learning about sales was experiential. I tend to steer clear of sales books like Dale Carnegie's *How to Win Friends and Influence People,* first published in 1937, but there's a fundamental reason some of them are among the top-selling books today. They are useful because they focus on essential ideas. And as I was interviewing for my first job out of Harvard Business School, when I said that I wanted part of my job to be in sales, that set me apart from many of the other business school graduates.

On Black Monday, Dell's deal got through not because investors were impressed with either me or Michael. We were working at the corporate level doing direct what Bill Spicer said I should be doing to start my career. We were selling PCs directly to customers. Michael and I used to listen in on those sales calls made from our offices at Headway Circle. We wanted to get a sense of the market. On those calls you could feel the market; you could hear what the customers were buying and what they weren't buying, what they were happy about. You could hear how our sales people were doing and where they were fumbling or stumbling. The power of being in direct touch with the market, especially one as dynamic as the PC market in the late 1980s, was huge.

CHAPTER 10

The Houseboat

When Michael started crying, I started crying.

It's true, it doesn't take much to get me going. But to be fair, this was a tough moment for both of us. By the spring of 1990 we'd done so much, been through so much in the four years since I accepted his offer to be president of his company. And we'd done it together in close partnership.

Michael told me he didn't want me to leave. I told him that I didn't want to leave but had no choice. I was too sick to continue at Dell.

Being president of Dell Computer had been a five-to-nine job. It required hard personnel decisions, financial attention, trade-offs, strategic direction, country-by-country implementation, and endless domestic tactical operational issues.

I had forgotten that I hadn't wanted to do this in the first place. I got caught up in the richness of a multidimensional puzzle, got swept up in the competitive fray of defeating IBM and Compaq. I forgot that once upon a time great clumps of my hair fell out and my back ached terribly when I was starting my own business. I ignored the possibility that I might be increasingly allergic to this kind of business activity. Did I believe that I was a tough South Texas guy, perhaps with a limited self-understanding, that I needed a catastrophic health problem to force myself from doing something I was temperamentally unsuited for over any extended period of time? I could handle the acids of the modern-day marketplace only in limited doses.

Michael and I were such different personalities. He was one of those business people who thrived on the stress of international high-tech competition. I was not. That impossibly complicated arena gave him energy. It had beaten me down to the point that I wasn't physically or emotionally strong enough to continue.

Now that the doctors had finally removed the implanted Groshong catheter that had been protruding from my chest for months, I had a lot of healing to do. I needed a bunch of stress-free recovery time. The uncomfortable Groshong device had been necessary to allow daily blood tests and infusions of different types of medical cocktails via the subclavian vein in my heart to treat the stubborn meningitis I had contracted.

The tipping point for me had been international travel. Over several years I had gone to Canada, England, France, Germany, and Sweden for the creation of our international subsidiaries. I did all this while serving as president of our domestic operation.

The moment of my collapse was etched in my mind. I had just returned to Austin after visiting our United Kingdom and German operations. While we now had a bunch of cash from our initial public offering, both Michael and I were still in the cash-conserving mode that had served us so well when we had little money.

We had decided that tourist-class air travel should be the standard for all of our executives, Michael and me included. As a result, I had contorted my six foot nine body into the cramped quarters of an eight-hour American Airlines flight from London to New York City and, after a short layover, had made the more than three-hour flight back to Austin tucked into a tight spot between two other weary business travelers.

After reaching Austin, I drove straightaway from the

airport to Dell's outdoor company-wide celebration. Upon arrival, I said a few words, bringing everyone up to speed on the company's international expansion. As I stepped down from the stage, I felt an excruciating pain in my lower back.

Soon after, I had back surgery at Brackenridge Hospital. After I came home, the pain returned with even greater intensity than before. Somewhere along the way I had picked up a form of meningitis that was to prove difficult to treat.

In the aftermath I had a strong recurring dream. I dreamed that I was floating in air, untethered from my heavy inert body, wafting free. I had this dream of being weightless so often that I began to imagine in my waking hours how I might make it come true.

The answer came out of the blue. I needed to live on a houseboat. I needed to float in water every day for as long as it took to heal. Even if it took several months, a year, several years. I needed to sleep at night on a good bed that rocked gently on quietly shifting waters. When I awoke, I needed to slowly lower myself into tree-shaded coves and paddle around. I needed to take long naps. When I got hungry I needed to pull into rustic marinas and eat while chatting up the locals.

I needed to be untethered—without phone, TV, radio, or anything electronic. I needed to be a child in nature again to give my body, mind, and spirit as much time as they needed to heal. To do that, I couldn't be president of Dell Computer Corporation anymore. I had no choice but to quit.

When I cry, I tend to weep miserable little tears. Michael's tears were something else, and he cried a lot when I told him it was my last day. I was deeply touched. His reaction told me he was grateful. He would miss me. I felt content. And I felt ready to move onto that houseboat.

The evening I met Michael four years earlier, I had been obsessed with an aging baseball player who had one too many

at bats, an older athlete who hadn't known when to quit. I
wasn't going to make that mistake. I wasn't worried about
whether I would be voted into some mythical hall of fame.
Somewhere along the way I decided this kind of bestowed
heroism didn't fundamentally matter.

I had some help in making my decision. My body
screamed that this was the right time for me, yelled so loudly
that I couldn't help but notice. My conscience was clear. Dell
Computer had a strong foundation and a promising future. I
could rest easy on my houseboat knowing that.

My time on the houseboat would start to give me the distance I needed. It's only in retrospect that I understand that
a forceful intervention made me shift my life onto a different
track.

On June 7 of that year I happened to pull my houseboat
into Hurst Harbor and saw on the TV news crowds of citizens
who had showed up to protest at an Austin City Council hearing. They were there to fight international mining and chem-
ical company Freeport McMoRan's proposal for a planned
unit development, or PUD, of 4,000 acres along the banks
of Barton Creek, an iconic Austin waterway intertwined with
the city's identity.

When I was nine years old, my family lived in a house
near a creek. On the other side of our house was an open
field where I kept my hideout, stocked with my homemade
bow, arrows, quiver, and secret touchstones. I splashed in my
creek at every chance, searched to find its headwaters, gorged
on the wild strawberries that grew on the opposite bank.
While we lived there for only two years before moving away,
that was the crucial formative time when I had the chance
to be a child in nature. At Hurst Harbor, watching my fellow
citizens rising up in protest, I wished I were there to help the
more than 900 people at that fourteen-hour-long city council

hearing, signing up to speak against the PUD that threatened
to pollute Barton Springs, a group of four natural springs
feeding into Barton Creek, and the larger Edwards Aquifer
underneath.

By the time I finally moved off the houseboat, a woman
named Brigid Shea had emerged as the leader of the Save
Our Springs (SOS) coalition. A native of South Dakota,
Brigid had been an award-winning journalist for National
Public Radio in Minnesota and Philadelphia before moving
to Austin in 1988 after reading a front-page story in the *New
York Times* about the congressional testimony given by Dr.
James E. Hansen, then director of NASA's Institute for Space
Studies. In his June 1988 testimony, Hansen asserted that he
was 99 percent certain that the continued use of fossil fuels
threatened the survival of the human race as well as millions
of other species on the planet. Hansen said that we were
approaching a tipping point when things would be taken out
of humanity's control.

Brigid later told me that the fact that Hansen spoke up
changed her life, and she decided to become more directly
involved in taking action herself. She moved to Austin that
same year to start the Texas chapter of Clean Water Action,
a national organization dedicated to environmental pro-
tection. Two years later, in 1990, she helped form SOS, a
citizen-driven initiative to protect Barton Springs against
unrestricted development in the Barton Creek watershed and
the product of the grassroots coalition formed shortly after
that all-night city council hearing on June 7, 1990.

I became aware of Brigid when I saw her during a televised debate in which she argued against those who felt that
an SOS ordinance limiting development, if passed, would
gravely damage the economy of Austin. Although she is
small in stature, she was a formidable presence, giving up no

ground during the debate. I also thought she had the better argument, and I asked if we could meet. We had lunch at a local restaurant less than a mile from Barton Springs, and I told her that I wanted to help any way I could.

At first, I brought doughnuts to sustain the hungry volunteers during their long meetings. As the group's strategy evolved, Brigid asked me if I would be willing to help with the SOS television ads. She said that since I was the first president of Dell Computer, I was seen as a business guy who could help give credibility to the cause because there were some, perhaps many, who saw SOS as just a bunch of whacked-out enviros. She asked, "Would you be willing to be the business face of our campaign on TV?"

A year earlier, actor and longtime environmentalist Robert Redford, who had learned to swim in the city park pool created by and named Barton Springs, agreed to make local radio ads to get the word out about the June 7 city council hearing. I was no Robert Redford, but, given Dell's success, I supposed I was the best available person for SOS to help legitimize itself. So my brief television ads aired regularly, where I said, "SOS, it's okay!"

The SOS tribe was one with whom I shared deep roots. My family's move to Austin in 1978 coincided with increasing highway construction and unrestricted development, which began to threaten the Central Texas water supply to Barton Springs. Always one to seek out tucked-away corners, whether at cocktail parties or in new cities, I had been drawn to a place called Westcave Preserve (now the Westcave Outdoor Discovery Center), a protected natural area about forty-five minutes outside of town. It sits on the edge of the Hill Country and overlooks the Pedernales River. Westcave's twenty-five acres existed around a natural grotto with a forty-foot waterfall. (It now sits on seventy-six acres to better protect it.) On my first visit there I met the late John Ahrns, who had been managing the preserve since 1974. He was good at sniffing out fellow tribal guys, and we bonded.

I soon learned that Westcave was in a precarious financial position. John Watson was a local architect who had provided the financing to buy the Westcave property, and he had hired John Ahrns to manage it. John Ahrns lived on-site with his wife, Brenda, and their two children, Jeff and Amber, in a used mobile home with a leaky roof. The two Johns had rescued the preserve from the developers' blade but had not figured out a sustainable business model for Westcave. I didn't know what that model should be, and it would take many years of thought and discussion by scores of dedicated people before we did figure it out. In the meantime, I felt my responsibility was to abide for however long it took, to cover personally the annual financial shortfall, and to never let John Ahrns defeat me in our many games of Horse in basketball.

John would walk ahead of me on the trail at Westcave, pointing out a Chinquapin oak tree or a bush honeysuckle and telling me to be careful where I put my oversized feet. "You can't be destroying things, so watch out," he told me. I had never thought about nature in quite that way before. I became a volunteer trail guide soon after, and I have to admit that I was pretty pathetic. I would fill in for John on weekends when he took off on camping trips with his family. I kept a blue book with the names, descriptions, and locations of the primary flora and fauna. I studied that book but never mastered the details about this tree or that flower, so visitors often corrected me. I was a poor substitute for John, but that's how I got started at Westcave, where I would end up serving almost three decades on its board.

There's no question that with my involvement in SOS, the

chief attraction was that I had been president of Dell. But I think I was also credentialed as an environmentalist because I had been involved with Westcave at that point for thirteen years, and today it's still the thing I've done the longest.

The SOS movement pushed many of my hot buttons. My sense of place, my sense of gratitude, my love of taking action on anything important to me. It was as if I could go back in time and try to help save my childhood creek, now paved over by a shopping center, the creek that had given me so many happy moments. While it was too late to save that boyhood creek of mine, I could join my fellow Austinites in trying to save our springs.

The coalition that had created Save Our Springs had collaborated to find a creative response to the threat to our place. As a South Texas boy at heart, I had never thought deeply about limiting what people could do on their property to protect the water supply beneath. My imagination was fired by the SOS group's audacity. And it was bold, their courage in taking on an issue so deep in the heart of Texas where property rights were regarded as sacrosanct, rights seen as virtually absolute. While it is true that Austin was far more liberal than any other city in Texas at the time, the working majority of the Austin City Council in the late 1980s was pro-development. Any opposition to this ethos was usually ad hoc and sufficiently divided to be ineffective. Save Our Springs was up against the Establishment, and for those of us who got organized, came up with an ordinance we wanted passed, and then actually got the ordinance passed, which required an election, it was a pretty big deal.

I was slow to understand how deep these feelings ran and would not begin to grasp their depth until I hit the campaign trail once the SOS ordinance had made it onto the ballot for the city's May 1992 election. I thought the ordinance, which limited the amount of land development within the Edwards Aquifer, offered a measured approach for development in and around the Barton Creek watershed. But for some people, the perceived loss of property value that Save Our Springs implied to them was something that triggered white-hot anger, boiling, fist-shaking rage. I knew enough about anger to recognize that many times it was the manifestation of fear. In this case something fundamental seemed threatened by SOS.

For me, it was a question of balancing multiple truths. In proposing alternate rules for future development over the Barton Creek watershed, we had to find a fair way through the competing interests of individual ownership, for which my conservative side had great sympathy, while not losing sight of our community's responsibility to protect the natural heritage of our Central Texas place, the stewardship of the bountiful gift we all enjoyed, this Hill Country of ours.

To me, this was civic engagement at its finest, citizens taking collective action when our elected representatives seemed slow to lead us in the right direction. The money men, the chamber of commerce, the city council, the state legislature, the leadership of Austin—all were lined up against SOS. Brigid Shea spent months collecting more than 30,000 signatures to put the ordinance on the ballot. It was classic creative disruption by a tribe of people committed to an important idea that was itself a feat of collaborative imagination coupled with outrageous courage in taking on the status quo and the sacred cow of absolute property rights, all in the middle of Texas, perhaps the most conservative state in our country.

This kind of citizen-led action happens so infrequently. But SOS used the tools of the opposing forces to limit them in their political reach. It was imagination in action, which isn't necessarily restricted to for-profit entities like Dell. In this case citizens dreamed up a collective solution, which is much harder to do than a couple of guys passing an inflatable globe back and forth. The boldness of citizens taking the lead like this blew my mind.

Thinking about the ingredients of place, imagination, and courage that had come together with SOS began to border on an obsession of mine. Not that I personally possessed any particular bravery myself, but with a growing understanding of gratitude, these were ideas I puzzled over constantly. All seemed to be converging within me as a philosophy, something to try to live my life by.

CHAPTER 11

The Denial of Death

We met in a corner.

I had just moved back to town after living on the house-boat. A friend had invited me to a cocktail party, and I made myself go to try to get back into the rhythm of social rituals.

I had just settled into a cozy corner when a stranger came gently jostling his way into my space. He asked me what I was doing in his corner. He asked with such sweet directness that all I could say was, "Holding it, saving it for you." He said that at cocktail parties he always headed for the corner because he found interesting people lurking there. And so we introduced ourselves.

His name was Warren Skaaren.

—○—

A few weeks went by. I was in Warren's apartment in South Austin. It was dark, squalid, depressing, surprising. How could someone who had written the screenplays for *Top Gun*, *Beetlejuice*, *Beverly Hills Cop II*, and *Batman*—movies grossing over a billion dollars, commercially some of the most success-ful in the history of cinema—how could he be living like this? Something didn't compute. I later learned that he and his wife had separated after twenty years of marriage. His health wasn't great. Like me, he had back issues. At forty-four, he was in the midst of a mid-life crisis; yet he was experiencing tremendous success in his professional life after the release a year earlier of *Batman*.

A few months after we first met, Warren called me saying his back pain had reached excruciating levels. Since back pain is what had ultimately led me to the houseboat, he wanted to know what advice I had. He was desperate. I said I thought I should come over. He said he wished I wouldn't. Okay, I said, but my healing magic was partially contingent on my touching his back with my giant hands.

My healing magic didn't work.

Despite my putting him through certain back exercises, helping him stretch out his hamstrings, changing out his soft, squishy sofa and bed, cleaning his fridge out of fatty food that was making his belly bigger, and laying my hands on his back in a way I had done for others—techniques that had never failed before—his suffering didn't go away. In fact, it got worse.

Soon after, at MD Anderson hospital in Houston, Warren was diagnosed with bone cancer and underwent surgery. When I heard this news, I drove to Houston on July 22, my birthday. Just before I arrived, his doctor told him he had six months left to live.

When I walked into Warren's hospital room, he waved me over to whisper something to me. He told me he needed my energy. Could I stay with him as much as possible? He had another friend, Tom Giebink. Maybe Tom and I could take turns? Of course, there would be twenty-four-hour nursing help and macrobiotic cooks making the nutritious meals that he hoped would help heal him, but he said he needed our energy around him.

"Please, say yes," he said.

—○—

The long nights were the worst. Cancer of the spine must be one of the most godawful afflictions because of its centrality, its core pain in the very middle of the sufferer's being. In those moments, there wasn't enough morphine on the planet to give Warren comfort. His screams made me want to bury my head in my hands, but that wasn't my job. My job was to be near him, help him shift into less painful positions, put ice-soaked cloths on his forehead, radiate my alleged energy aura.

"Tell me about Yugoslavia," he said.

I told him about Dubrovnik, Sarajevo, and Belgrade and about exploring the Danube River in an old wooden, flat-bottomed boat that my Yugoslavian friend, Nemanya, had scrounged up somehow. Nemanya and I spent many happy days in the summer of 1963 paddling in and out of the nooks of the enormous Danube, staying mostly on its west side because we feared the tricky, sweeping currents in its vast middle.

I told Warren that Nemanya had named his little boat *Bogomil*, which means "dear God" in Slavic and was the name of a now-disappeared religious Gnostic sect that began in the Balkans in the tenth century. Warren asked me to repeat the boat's name. When I did, he was incredulous. He asked if I had ever seen *Beverly Hills Cop II*. I had not.

For a moment, Warren's pain from cancer was forgotten. I had stumbled across one of the trip wires in Warren's immense store of imaginative esoterica. Warren, who had been hired to rewrite *Beverly Hills Cop II* so that it could go in front of the cameras, said he had given the name Bogomil to the detective who was nearly killed in the movie. He found the name in one of the many obscure reference books in his collection and thought it would be a good name for a detective. Warren's writing talent and his exceptional listening skills helped him become a successful screenwriter, but it was his wide-ranging curiosity and fertile imagination that kept him in demand. People liked being around such an interesting guy, and Hollywood thrives on relationships. Stars like Tom Cruise and Michael Douglas enjoyed working with Warren because he was a smart writer and an interesting person.

Another time, I told Warren about living in Sweden and Denmark, about my successful search for the gravesite of UN secretary-general and Nobel Peace Prize winner Dag Hammarskjöld. Warren didn't care about Dag Hammarskjöld, but when I mentioned my unsuccessful search for Søren Kierkegaard's gravesite (I got diverted by a young woman named Vera Riddespore), Warren became excited and demanded that I tell him everything about that visit.

Once again, I had tripped over a wire attached to Warren's peculiar tastes. He asked me why I had been looking for Kierkegaard's gravesite. I told him it was because of Kierkegaard's possible influence over theoretical physicist Niels Bohr when Bohr formed his thoughts about the wave/particle nature of light. After all, I had been a physics major and Niels Bohr was one of my icons. Warren's face relaxed into a smile. What I didn't know at the time was that Søren Kierkegaard was the subject of a chapter in *The Denial of Death,* a Pulitzer Prize–winning book by Ernest Becker, which, I would come to find out later, had special meaning for Warren. Becker wrote about our "mechanisms of defense" such as repression and denial. Kierkegaard talked about the same things using different terms: he thought that most people live in "half-obscurity" about their own condition, a state of "shut-upness" wherein they block off their own perceptions of reality.

These moments of respite and pleasure didn't happen very often. As day after night after day slogged by, Warren grew weaker and weaker. Toward the end, Warren's agony intensified, but we had one last moment when he seemed to forget his pain.

Making small talk, I said I had just received an offer to teach at the University of Texas in the upcoming summer session, a six-week engagement on a syllabus yet to be developed. I hadn't realized the topic of UT was another hot button for Warren. He told me that they would eat me alive, that I was unbelievably gullible, and that UT was a den of tricksters and intrigue.

Tim Ruefli, from the McCombs School of Business, had called wondering if I would like to teach a summer class for a group of MBA candidates. He knew that I had been president of Dell, and he needed someone to teach at the last minute. I asked Tim what he thought I should teach them. He said he guessed my course would have something to do with management, given my experience at Dell and my previous entrepreneurial career. I told him I didn't even know what to call the course. Tim mentioned that he thought we were about to go to war with Iraq. He suggested the title "Frontline Management."

I liked the name but worried that I might not have much to teach. Tim laughed and said that it didn't matter if I fell flat on my face, which he doubted would happen. The course lasted only six weeks; it would be over in a blink.

Six months later I was standing in front of twenty-five students. When the first class was over, one of them, John Harris, approached me and said that he had come to UT to get an MBA, not a philosophy degree. That day's class had felt like a philosophy class to him. He apologized, saying that if that first class was representative of what the course was going to be, maybe he should switch to something else. We were both a bit embarrassed.

I told John that I would hate to lose him, that this was my first day ever of teaching, that there were bound to be some rough patches. I told him that I hoped he would stay, but I understood if he felt like he needed to transfer. John Harris gave me a disappointed look and then shuffled away.

It was a trying first day.

Driving home later, I wondered why I had thought it was a good idea to teach my first and probably only college class based on the book *The Denial of Death*. I decided it was all Warren Skaaren's fault, even though he had died six months earlier.

I had been there when he passed away in late December 1990 and again not long after when our friend Amon Burton found a dozen or so copies of *The Denial of Death* on Warren's bookshelf. "It was his favorite book," Amon said. That's funny, I thought to myself at the time. We talked about everything except Warren's favorite book. His last few months were a total denial of *The Denial of Death*.

I suppose it matters a lot when and where we read certain books. For example, I first read Somerset Maugham's *Of Human Bondage* when I was twenty-one, while lolling around on the beaches of the Danube River in Yugoslavia. I identified completely with the club-footed Philip as he searched for the meaning of life while pursuing Mildred, who treated him like dirt. I remember slowing down as I approached the last page to better savor every last morsel. And as I finished Maugham's classic, I knew this was the greatest book ever written. Many years later in a different place, I reread *Of Human Bondage* and changed my opinion.

But as I read *The Denial of Death* after Warren's death, several ideas struck me with great force. Becker's insight about our being born in obscurity, dying in oblivion, and not making any difference in our lives in between was especially poignant. Warren had died at the age of forty-four, the same age as my father when he passed away in 1962. They both died of cancer, and neither was ready to die.

I thought, this can't be a coincidence. I'm desperate for some central theme to teach this summer, and the universe has delivered this book, a final gift from Warren. Much later I would learn that he had discovered the book in the mid-1970s. He had been working on a screenplay about the University of Texas football player Freddie Steinmark, a senior who had helped lead the team to a national championship in 1969. Just days after the game, Steinmark was diagnosed with bone cancer, underwent surgery soon after, and passed away two years later. Heroism. That was it. I would teach my MBA students everything I knew or thought I knew about heroism.

And then on my first day of teaching John Harris told me he wasn't coming back, and I bet he wasn't the only one. Probably half my class would desert me. And for good reason. Why would anyone getting an MBA degree suffer through thirty boring lectures on what to them was probably an obscure book called *The Denial of Death*? I myself would have paid money to avoid a class like that when I was getting my MBA.

I'm not sure I realized at the time the full impact that Warren's unexpected death had on me. We had struck up a brief but intense friendship, and then he was gone. My confused emotional perspective seemed to dictate my choosing that one book as a way to focus the class.

I drove home that day and knew that I needed to make a change before the second class meeting the next day. When it comes to entrepreneurship, I have no problem staying up all night and changing my business model, and that's what I did my first summer of teaching. *The Denial of Death* was not, after all, going to be the focus of my first course.

More than two decades have passed since I taught that first class. John Harris decided not to drop the course, and at the end of it he and the other students presented me with their "Hero of the Year" award. Each student had signed his or her name to a certificate given to me for "excellence in teaching, listening, and storytelling during his rookie season." Today it hangs framed on my office wall.

And even though I no longer teach in the business school, I do include Warren's work and the concept of courage in my Plan II Honors syllabus. Every semester I take my class to the Harry Ransom Center, an archive of rare books, manuscripts, and other documents that make up the collections of writers like Arthur Miller, Carlo Levi, J. Frank Dobie, John Graves, and, yes, Warren Skaaren. What draws me to these writers whose work we examine is that they all seemed to harness their imaginations to a cause. I think most of us are not brave people. But if we find a cause we're interested in and can put our imaginations to work on that cause, then we forget to be scared. Was Carlo Levi, who was Italian and Jewish, just naturally brave or did he find his courage in his hatred of Fascism?

I am not ashamed to admit that I include Warren's archive, which has his scripts and notes for *Batman*, because I teach millennials, and I think this film may speak to them more readily than Miller's play *Death of a Salesman* or Graves's book *Goodbye to a River*. I also think it's important to consider what faux heroes teach us. Perhaps superhero franchises are so popular because human beings need to be inspired. We are fearful creatures who marvel (pun intended) at the selfless audacity of superheroes like Batman, Superman, and Wonder Woman.

Warren hadn't wanted me to teach at UT. What he didn't tell me then was that before he became one of Hollywood's top screenwriters, he had desperately wanted to teach at the university. A class had become available, but they had given it to another aspiring screenwriter instead of Warren. When I told him about Ruefli's offer, he was adamant that I would be taken advantage of. He asked me to go into his rock garden and bring back a stone. I went into the garden, found a stone that I liked, and returned to his side. He took my pebble, mumbled some barely audible blessings over it, and then handed it back to me saying, "Lee, keep this stone near you, especially when you're at UT. And whenever someone is talking to you, you are to rub this stone and say to yourself, 'What I'm hearing may not be true.'"

I've still got Warren's stone.

CHAPTER 12

The Lambkin Society

"Ms. Salazar, is your balance sheet correct?"

"Yes, sir. Well, I hope so."

"How much inventory will you need?" I asked.

She began to thumb through her papers and then looked up.

"I think . . . I think we forgot the inventory line," she said in a barely audible voice.

"Forgot the inventory?"

"Yes, sir . . . I'm afraid so."

"How can you have a manufacturing business without inventory?"

"We can't. We made a mistake."

There was a stir in the student audience. They were squirming in their chairs as their classmate went down in flames, some of them thinking "there but for the grace of God go I." They were watching the finals of the Moot Corp Competition to find out which MBA team would win the best business plan in the university's annual new venture competition for graduate students.

"Ms. Salazar, you need to correct your balance sheets. You're going to need more money than you're showing."

"Yessir," her voice trailed off, her face miserable, pale.

"Maybe a lot more money?"

"Yessir, maybe . . ."

I paused, wondering if I should stop my cross-examination. Had I turned into what I feared and disliked so much when I was an MBA student? Twenty-five years earlier, Harvard

professor John McNaughton had given me the gift of kindness and mercy without which I would have failed business
school. Now here I was beating up this student because she
had forgotten . . . inventory. Had Professor McNaughton done
anything like this to me, I would have stuck my head in an
oven and lit a match.

"Thank you, Ms. Salazar. No more questions."

—◇—

That first summer of teaching, when I came back for my
second day of class, I was relieved to find all twenty-five of my
students still there, including John Harris, who had protested
that he hadn't come to business school to take a philosophy
course. I'd been up most of the night trying to figure out what
to do.

The only thing I knew was entrepreneurship, and all I
could think of was to tell stories. Before I had become Dell's
first president, I had started various companies, succeeding
at some, some not. While unpleasant, my Harvard Business
School experience had shown me a way to teach by pre-
senting case studies of business successes and failures. By
studying these cases, we learned the strategies that worked
and why others did not.

What if I emphasized storytelling when I presented the
cases?

The stories I knew well were my own stories. I began to
write them down, starting with my own pathetic beginnings
in business when a ninety-four-year-old man wearing a tie
had cheated me out of most of my money.

Then I wrote another story of how I had scrambled and
scraped and, with a combination of luck and daring, had
somehow muddled through my earliest business ventures
against all odds.

Then I wrote another story of how my business competitors suddenly panicked, thinking I was bigger and stronger than I really was, and of how they suddenly sold me their business at a price I couldn't refuse. I wrote another story of how bankers started bringing me companies in distress because I was getting a reputation for being an honorable person in making my business deals.

More stories followed. I wrote about helping to start a venture capital company and about helping a young college dropout perfect his business model, which turned into one of the largest corporations in the world.

All of these stories were charged with the excitement of genuine entrepreneurship. They were narratives of someone stumbling along at first but gathering momentum as he learned the trade. They were stories that suggested to my students that if this guy could do these things, maybe they could, too. I wrote each of my stories as a business case, always with this question: "What should Mr. Walker do and why should he do it?"

These stories had a certain universality, revealing a young person trying to sort out and make his way in the world, trying to figure out what was true and what wasn't, trying to determine what was a good deal and what wasn't, and trying to be fair and equitable in a world that sometimes didn't seem to respond in kind or very kindly.

Stephen Covey's *The 7 Habits of Highly Effective People* had been published a couple of years earlier. What if I organized my class around seven ideas or perspectives on business management—the important points of reference I had used as tools in coping with the complexities I faced in the business world?

I decided to stick with the idea of heroism. Imagination was an obvious choice, as was numeracy. I needed to flesh out

the other four. While recuperating on the houseboat, I had
read Annie Dillard's *The Writing Life*. In it she writes about
the importance of schedules and choosing how to spend
one's time. A schedule, Dillard writes, "defends from chaos
and whim." She describes it as "a net for catching days" and
"a haven set into the wreck of time." So I added a course
perspective on scheduling. I also included one called "paying
attention." I had noticed that the best entrepreneurs, particularly at the front end of an endeavor, paid attention better
than most people. Michael Dell, for instance, paid attention
better than anybody I'd ever seen. I was charmed and amused
to discover how much Michael had observed after one visit
to a supplier. Michael was a master at reading documents
upside down and at a distance on people's desks, and he had
an uncanny ability to glean important information with this
skill.

The ability to help people became another course perspective. I struggled a bit before settling on the last one—criticism. I was intrigued by its old-fashioned meaning and by
the way literary theories might increase students' capacity to
think critically without bias or prejudice. I was interested in
how MBA students might be able to gain additional insight if
encouraged to develop critical thinking skills. Critical thinking gets us past our -isms, our cultural identities, our mind-
sets. In 1977 the president of Digital Equipment Corporation
(DEC), one of the world's largest and most successful computer companies, told an audience that there was no reason
for any individual to have a computer in his or her home. He
was a smart guy, but this was his mind-set, and ultimately it
prevented DEC from succeeding in the computer industry.

I would embed within my stories perspective lessons in
heroism, imagination, numeracy, scheduling, paying attention, helping, and criticism. But my business case stories

were also chock-full of financial information, requiring students to wrestle with questions located at the intersection of numbers and narrative. And along with the stories and the lessons, I tried to bring something else into my classroom: a safe place.

The model at Harvard was deliberately Darwinian, designed to weed out the weakest of us. To those of us who were dead broke, it piled on, and it was measuredly non-nurturing to the shy. What would happen, I wondered, if I combined the case method approach with kindness toward those students who were naturally shy, as I had been while at Harvard? In that spirit, what if I as the teacher coaxed my students rather than humiliated them?

It didn't take me long to figure out who the quiet and timid students were, students like me when I was in business school.

In that class in the summer of '91, there were seven: Cami, Bradley, Amanda, Amit, Cynthia, Mahesh, and William. Seven out of a total of twenty-five students—28 percent of my class—were introverts who had revealed themselves.

I invited all seven of them to my office. What would happen if they formed a mutual support club? What would happen if they exulted in their quietness, celebrated their introversion? What if they formed a club called the Lambkin Society?

And what if they made me, their professor, an honorary member of their club? While I no longer fainted from fear when speaking in public, I still had, and I supposed always would have, anxieties. Where was it written that a professor couldn't be a Lambkin, too? I had first discovered the word while reading a speech by the bragging soldier Pistol in Shakespeare's *Henry IV*, and I was charmed by its reference to tender young innocents.

Not just anybody could join our society. You had to be the
real deal—no faking, no pretending. You had to be a genuine
namby-pamby, dedicated to your quiet ways.

We discussed what it meant to be a Lambkin. I asked if
each would be willing to put his or her hand up in every class
during our class discussions, if each of them in every class
would be willing to ask at least one question, any question.
Just ask something. Finally, all the Lambkins agreed. Each
would find one single something to say in every class.

I was obsessed with making my class a safe place for
learning. The dangerous places of the world would soon be
upon them.

CHAPTER 13

The Rail Not Taken

I am cruising through the University of Texas campus, riding in one of Austin's sleek, high-tech, light-rail trains as it makes its way from the neighborhoods just north of campus to downtown, where the city's new central branch of the public library overlooks the shores of Lady Bird Lake. The limestone facades of the university buildings slide by as the train leaves the campus area and heads toward the State Capitol. Undergraduate and graduate students, visible from the train's windows, give way to legislators and lobbyists shuffling between their offices in nearby state buildings and the Capitol. The scenery outside my train window changes again as we leave the Capitol station and head into Austin's downtown core. With UT's 110,000 ingresses and egresses a day, the 50,000 at the Capitol, and the exploding number downtown, the light-rail system knits together the Austin community.

And yet this is all in my imagination. The conveyor-belt type transit route that I had envisioned for Austin's central core never came to pass during my eleven years as chairman of Capital Metro, Central Texas' transit agency. The proposal for a light-rail route in Austin was on the ballot for the 2000 election. I had been in the volunteer position as chair since 1997, juggling it along with my part-time teaching at UT.

The original business model failed on the 2000 ballot, but it was a narrow defeat. As the election returns came in that November evening, we were winning. I had more than

one person come over and say, "Looks like you got your rail."
It was too soon to celebrate, but it did look hopeful. Central
Austin voters seemed to be supporting light rail, but in the
peripheral areas around Austin—Jonestown, Leander, and
other areas to the north, south, and east—their returns were
coming in much slower than those for Central Austin. But
as the evening wore on, you could just see the erosion of that
win.

The next morning the headline on the front page of the
Austin American-Statesman newspaper read, "Bush wins,
light rail still hanging in the balance." This election, of
course, was about more than just light rail. It was also a presidential contest, and in reality the opposite of the *Statesman's*
headline was true. The presidential election would hang in
the balance for weeks, but light rail's fate had been decided.
We had lost by fewer than 2,000 votes, or less than one
percent. In the aftermath, I thought seriously about resign-
ing. I had led us to defeat and felt terrible about my failure.
I thought the tides were running against light rail: voters in
the car-reliant suburbs were gaining clout, opposition toward
the idea seemed to be mounting, and politics in general was
polarizing.

But maybe we could reframe our argument. I came to
the conclusion that we had to find a better business model
because the one we had wasn't working. We realized we
needed to redefine our argument around the Envision
Central Texas movement, a nonprofit organization made up
of business leaders, neighborhood representatives, policy-
makers, and environmental organizers who came together
in 2002 to work on a plan for the area's proposed growth.
This reframing led to a light-rail victory in 2004, a citizen-led
success, a success born out of a framing of what was at stake,
a different set of lenses to see a different future.

As we were losing the vote that November evening in 2000, I thought back to a meeting I had had with student leaders from the university. My fellow UT professor Austin Gleeson, who taught in the physics department, was a big supporter of transit. He and I decided to meet with members of the editorial board of the *Daily Texan,* UT's student newspaper, at the Hole in the Wall, a popular dive just north of campus. We had heard that the student editors were leaning toward a vote of no confidence on the transit proposal, and we hoped to change their minds. This didn't happen. The opposition's argument that light rail would cost too much and do too little had won them over. Early polls were showing the proposal with only a narrow margin. We couldn't afford to lose support in the center of the city, which included the university. On election night as we watched the returns come in and I began to realize that the vote was not going to pass, I thought about the power involved in that meeting and what could have been.

But I also remember thinking about the unfairness of that Hole in the Wall meeting. The sensibility about place and built environments that I expected the student leaders to grasp was something that had taken me several years to comprehend. To paraphrase Winston Churchill, "We shape our places; thereafter they shape us." It is a complicated idea, and it took me a long time to understand it. The idea that we could turn someone's thinking around in one sitting wasn't fair to the student leaders. Talk about a lack of imagination: it never occurred to me to have a series of meetings to explain our position because it never occurred to me that the student leaders wouldn't be on board with the proposal the way the student community had been with the Save Our Springs initiative a decade earlier. In my mind, SOS and the proposal for light rail were nearly identical. They both had to do with the built environment and its effect on our quality of life in Austin.

Activist and urban studies pioneer Jane Jacobs begins her book *The Death and Life of Great American Cities* with a bold statement: "This book is an attack on current city planning and rebuilding." Jacobs writes about how citizens generally don't get involved in city planning issues until it's too late. Most people don't question things like a city's decision to put a road in a particular place until the road in question goes right through their own house. I took this to heart.

How did an entrepreneur and teacher who dislikes public speaking end up overseeing Central Texas' transit agency? When I was a boy, I spent my summers with my maternal grandparents, Fred and Prudence Baker, whose small house at 1520 South Broadway sat close to the Kansas City Southern railroad tracks in Pittsburg, Kansas. I remember hobos coming off the train tracks and showing up at the back door to the kitchen, where my tiny grandma would make sandwiches for them from whatever leftovers were around. When I was eight years old, my grandparents let me start riding the bus by myself downtown to the Colonial Theatre, where I fell in love with movie stars like Margaret Sullavan, Jean Arthur, and Greer Garson. To this day, I watch their movies over and over again.

Sometimes I'd take the crosstown bus to Lincoln Park, where I'd sit in the kiddie pool (I never learned to swim) and watch closely for hours on end as mothers dipped and splashed their children. My moxie and sense of self-reliance grew as I came to know the bus drivers and be patted on the shoulder by some of the other frequent riders. I listened as they talked about the Korean War and I wondered how it could be possible for soldiers so far away to have babies in their wives' arms in the seat right next to me.

So in 1996, when Austin's local paper began reporting on scandals at Capital Metro, it ignited my own personal recollections of taking the bus to downtown Pittsburg as a boy, of taking the train to midtown Manhattan as a young man, and of taking trains and buses all over Europe and Africa as I gallivanted around in the years between these memories. *Statesman* reporter Laylan Copelin wrote nonstop exposés of what was going on at Cap Metro. Copelin's investigative reporting, a bit of a lost art, probed and explained the corruption at Cap Metro. The essence of that corruption was sweetheart deals for bogus work. The taxpayer side of me was outraged as I read Laylan's pieces. The scandal-loving, lurid side of me was titillated. I smacked my lips over the details. The academic side of me was curious about why the governance system at the agency had failed. The civic entrepreneur side of me knew about Austin's historical doubling of its population every twenty years. We were headed toward a choke point, and an enfeebled transit agency would be hard-pressed to meet that demand.

In the end, the Texas Legislature fired the entire Cap Metro board of directors in order to create a new, seven-member board. Certain friends gently and persistently nudged me to help out by applying for one of the two at-large positions. I didn't want to. It felt alien, too governmental for entrepreneurial me. It felt foreign to my secret self that was frightened by being on a public stage, scary to that part of me that prefers sitting on my front porch in my rocking chair reading a book.

But I loved Austin and by that time had been living there for almost twenty years after getting back to Texas from the Northeast. I had known from my high school days when I traveled to Austin for a math competition that one day I would commit to the city, a good place to grow old, I thought, a good place to be near my friends and family, a place with libraries galore.

Cars and trains per se don't interest me, but transit's potential to connect people and places does. Cap Metro was a cause that nudged me.

Still, it was tough to work at Cap Metro some days. It felt hard because of its complexity. It was always a balancing act between the riders, who needed more routes and buses, and our workers and drivers, who wanted better pay and health insurance. There seemed to be many constituencies, and everything had to be evaluated through a political prism. One of the things I liked about running Cap Metro was hearing from Austin's citizens during meetings in which they could share input about the city's transit system. It gave me a chance to be respectful of their opinions and to try to respond. I also enjoyed what I called my "secret shopping" trips, when I would ride the bus up and down Guadalupe Street, known as the Drag where it runs through the UT campus, to get a sense of how the bus routes were working and what the public thought of the agency. To me the buses were overcrowded, and they didn't run with sufficient periodicity. We tried to address these issues during my eleven years as chairman of Cap Metro.

This work eventually influenced the way I taught my classes at UT. Today I take my students on many field trips throughout the semester. There's something about human beings needing to experience things directly: Our imaginations alone can take us only so far.

My students and I take the Capital MetroRail train from downtown Austin to the Martin Luther King station on the east side of the city. I want my students to see that transit-taking is for everyone. We take a bus to the Triangle, a walkable, mixed-use development just north of the university that came into being with help from students just like them. The Triangle area also was designed to be a Park 'n Ride, although Austin's light rail hasn't expanded to take advantage of that station yet. I take my students to the Triangle so they can see a glimpse of the future—the future of transit and quite possibly their future, when they might be as galvanized as UT students and siblings Charles and Sabrina Burmeister were when they rallied the neighborhoods to come up with a plan that eventually became the Triangle.

In the early 2000s Charles and Sabrina were fond of playing with their dog on a triangle of green space just north of 45th Street while throwing their Frisbee or sitting under a favorite tree to read. Officials for the state, under severe economic pressure, were determined to make some money from this land and were dismissive of the students. My wife Jen and I were involved with our neighborhood association, and this piece of land bordered our neighborhood. When the students came to us for help, my immediate answer was no, just as it had been for Michael Dell when he first came to my home on Cat Mountain. The Burmeisters' fight against the state—and I knew enough about state politics to know it would be a fight—seemed impractical.

But Jen and I became annoyed at what seemed to be the disdainful way the state officials were treating the students, so we decided to jump in. What followed was a student-led movement that gathered thousands of signatures on a petition opposing the State of Texas' plan to create a suburban-style shopping center that would have included a giant asphalt parking lot.

I was certain we would lose but felt it was important to give the state a tussle as a matter of civic duty, something like when baseball managers argue with the umpire at home plate. They know nothing will change but hope that, the next time around, maybe the ump will remember that moment and try to make a better call.

Efforts like ours usually fail because it's not enough to simply oppose something. There has to be an alternative to what's being proposed. So we made a different proposal, an alternate aspiration to all that asphalt, which included a mixed-use development with wide sidewalks and narrow streets, living spaces located above retail shops, large swatches of green space where someday there might be a weekly farmer's market and where movies could be shown on a large outdoor screen. Nearby would be bocce courts for the old, splash pads for the kids, and spaces wide and green enough for everyone to throw Frisbees and play with their dogs.

A collaboration between neighborhoods, inspired and led by Sabrina and Charles, ultimately became the Triangle project, one of the most vibrant and economically robust parts of Austin. It is a fine example of imagination in action and was one of the first expressions of the New Urbanism movement in Austin.

Every summer when I speak to incoming A&M freshmen in Italy, I talk about their field trips to cities like Florence and Rome. I describe the concept of cathedral thinking, a term whose medieval roots date back to a time when artisans and builders came together to imagine what the great cathedrals would look like and to create plans, blueprints, and schedules to build them. These projects took years, even decades, to complete, and some of the people who helped to create them weren't even around to see them once they were finished.

I also point out how Italians in general handle their built environment differently. Cars are sharply restricted, for example, to preserve the walkability of the cities and towns. This reminds me of an ongoing project at the University of

Texas to close off to cars a busy thoroughfare that borders the northern boundary of the campus. In 2002 Austin Gleeson, my wife Jen, and I met with then-UT president Larry Faulkner about the possibility. Jen and I had always been interested in public spaces and places, and we had worked diligently for traffic calming measures in our own Hyde Park neighborhood just north of UT. Austin Gleeson asked us to meet with him and the university president to discuss the possibility of closing off Speedway Avenue. Sixteen years later, the effort is complete. It winds through campus like Oz's Yellow Brick Road.

This example illustrates the long time frames required for such projects, particularly when they involve collaboration with a large institution like a major university in a fast-growing capital city in the second-largest state in the country. These long time frames seem to discourage student involvement in particular. There is an asymmetry between the tight time frames in which students operate—semesters, four years at most—and the length of time it takes to work out solutions to complex civic issues.

I want my students to begin to grasp the fundamental relationship between place and transit, between geography and connection, between how we develop our land and how we live with one another and with ourselves. I want my students to think about what things will look like 100 years from now.

Even as I write this, I can see that as a society we're moving beyond the conventional, automobile-centric model. Autonomous, electric cars will create a tectonic shift in how we think about transit. Current studies discuss mobility as a service, and this move away from a car-centric culture will have implications for the built environment. There's a need to fundamentally redesign our cities using forward-thinking urban design. It will involve a complete overhaul of how we think about our cities, and it will incorporate electric-based, autonomous mobility in cities properly designed for it.

What I find exciting now is that we're starting to understand it's all about our fundamental need for connection. It's not about the train. It's not about the electric car. It's about the place catalyzed by these advances and about our human need to be connected with each other.

CHAPTER 14

The Imagination House

"Do you have any questions?"

Apparently, they did not. An audience of sleek young athletic Nike executives sat in what seemed like stunned silence. They had come to Austin from Beaverton, Oregon, in 2004 for a three-day brainstorming session to be held in what my wife Jen and I called our Imagination House, a tiny faded pink stucco structure tucked away in the Hyde Park neighborhood just north of the University of Texas.

The Nike team was led by Scott MacEachern, the founder and general manager of the Nike Livestrong partnership, who had been wanting to have a retreat at our Imagination House from the first time he saw it. I worried that it was much too tiny and inadequate for huge Nike. But Scott insisted. "I love its energy," he said.

So did I. The collaborative imagination of my wife Jen, our neighbor Carol Burton, with her subtle sense of color and design, and acclaimed architect Robert Jackson had dreamed up a magical place that was so much more than the sum of its parts. The space itself was only 500 square feet, but it had giant doors, abundant windows, a ceiling that soared twenty feet, a warm inviting fireplace, and a whiteboard-covered wall that encouraged imagination and creativity.

Scott believed that Nike could help make Livestrong, formerly the Lance Armstrong Foundation, into one of the finest not-for-profit enterprises in the world. To do that, Scott wanted to get his team down to Austin to get their minds fully engaged. He wanted me to begin with a talk about imagination.

I said yes to Scott's request. At that point I was chairman of Livestrong. It wasn't hard to see the vast potential in a strong connection to Nike. From its modest beginning in 1964, when Phil Knight and his track coach Bill Bowerman had launched it, Nike had grown into a behemoth. Nike as a partner was something that fledgling not-for-profits like Livestrong dreamed about.

But now that I had finished my talk, the Nike gang was mute. I had told them three stories: about the invention of Dell Computer Company's service and support, which helped catapult the company into Fortune 500 status; how the citizens of Austin had created the Save Our Springs movement, helping to make our hometown one of America's most attractive cities to live in; and how we in our Hyde Park neighborhood had saved the back alleys that connected us to one another when Austin city officials deemed them ineffi-cient for trash pick-up. To me, these three stories showcased the power of collaborative imagination in the for-profit and not-for-profit worlds.

This wasn't the first time that a speech of mine had bombed. The good news was that it was over and done with. As I turned to Scott, I saw a feeble gesture from the back of the room. I wasn't sure if the Nike executive had a question or if he was gently swatting away a bug.

"How old are you?" he asked.

"I'm sixty-five," I said.

The room fell silent. As I turned once again to Scott, I saw the same young man's hand wave with a bit more energy. He asked me how I felt about being sixty-five years old. It occurred to me that maybe what I needed to do was to take his question and find a way to stretch out my answer.

How did I feel about being sixty-five? I decided to go

mathematical. I said that 65 was 13 times 5, and that 13 was a terribly important Fibonacci number, named for the Italian mathematician Leonardo Fibonacci, who stated that the sum of any two consecutive numbers in a particular series equals the next highest number. I told the group that I could describe my life to that point in five distinct thirteen-year stages. My first thirteen years had been my formative years of learning perfectly the Catholic Baltimore catechism and Latin mass while memorizing great swaths of baseball statistics and playing outdoors. My second thirteen had been about launching rockets, studying physics, math, and Russian, playing basketball, soaking up foreign cultures, and suffering at Harvard. My third thirteen had been my entrepreneurial years of trying to make money. I told them that my fourth thirteen had been my fumbling-around, waiting-to-die years because I suspected I would die young like my father did. But since that hadn't happened, I had jammed in four years at Dell Computer before getting terribly sick, then living on a houseboat to recover. My fifth thirteen had been a time of teaching entrepreneurship at the University of Texas while jumping into community issues that caught my fancy. That brought me to age sixty-five, on the cusp of beginning my sixth thirteen-year period. I told the Nike group I was intrigued about its possibilities. I was especially fascinated about what my seventh thirteen might have waiting for me, should I be given the gift of the ages seventy-eight to ninety-one, because I thought that period would be the time of my operating at the peak of my imaginative powers. Of course, all these future possibilities were predicated on my not being run over by a Capital Metro bus or fatally falling off my bike or even slipping on a soap bar in the shower.

I took a breath. The room seemed suddenly alive, animated. Many hands shot up into the air. While I don't remember the next question, the conversation that followed was just what Scott and I had been hoping for. Over the next three days a burst of invention put the partnership of Livestrong and Nike into hyperdrive, creating an extraordinary example of profit/not-for-profit collaboration. How often does a fledgling, entrepreneurial not-for-profit match up with a Fortune 500 company to produce a truly equitable partnership in which each side brings substance to the table? Livestrong had an extraordinary cause around cancer, a disease that affects every community around the globe, and its focus on survivorship tapped into an incredible amount of energy. The Livestrong-Nike collaboration's most visible result has been, of course, the yellow silicone gel bracelet that raised more than $80 million for cancer research.

The Nike gang in our Imagination House had needed just a pinch of time to get their mental engines revved up. And perhaps the spontaneous riff I did about my quirky approach to the stages of my life had struck a chord with these driven executives under constant pressure to succeed and deliver. In my ad lib response about how it felt to be sixty-five years old, I had dreamed up the mental scaffolding as I thought about the sixth thirteen that was upon me. I was thought-playing within the Imagination House, a physical space that had been designed to spark playfulness. It was a kind of reframing of the Nike executive's question, in my experience the most useful tool when dealing with pressure. And maybe my off-the-cuff remarks made the Nike executives wonder if they didn't have more choices in their personal and career lives. Lots more choices. If I have a central mantra, it is that we invariably underimagine our possibilities.

Essentially, I was proposing that maybe, contrary to some scientific research, imagination was the one faculty that defied aging. Articles such as "Age-Related Changes in the

Episodic Simulation of Future Events" in *Psychological Science* suggest that we have less capacity to imagine as we age, but I wonder if imagination has the possibility of being enriched by age and experience. If imagination is about choices, I see so many more ways of dealing with life now than I did at ages thirteen, twenty-six, thirty-nine, and so on.

While I'm willing to concede that the imagination of the younger mind frequently outshines that of the older person, the Nike-Livestrong meeting at our Imagination House is a perfect example of how imaginative collaboration across age groups can be so powerful.

Some weeks after the Nike meeting Scott called me and asked if we could meet at Magnolia Café, a local twenty-four-hour restaurant. Scott was sitting on the bench in front when I pulled up. I sat next to him and he handed me a big box. Inside the box were a set of Nike Air Force One sneakers, the company's best-selling line up to that point. When I took them out of the box, I saw imprinted in gold on the side a series of 13s. The first five 13s were emblazoned in gold. The sixth 13 had just a smidge of gold at its base. I keep these shoes near my desk. Someday I'll find a good occasion to wear them. In the meantime, they're a daily reminder to me of the power of imagination.

—◇—

In October 1996 Lance Armstrong invited me over for dinner, soon after he had been diagnosed with cancer and a few years before he was the famous seven-time winner of the Tour de France.

"What do you think?" Lance asked across the dinner table. Lance had told me how he had just heard from some-one named Dr. Steven Wolff at Vanderbilt University. Wolff was an avid bicyclist and had read a news clip about Lance's testicular cancer. Wolff thought Lance should take a look at the Indiana University Cancer Center for treatment even though Lance had been considering MD Anderson in Houston.

"Indiana?" I thought. How could that be better than MD Anderson? Lance explained that Dr. Wolff thought the Indiana Cancer Center's latest research in testicular cancer might be a better answer, might give him better odds of survival, and if he survived, might better preserve his bicycling career.

"What do you think I should do?" Lance repeated.

What should he do? I had no idea. My six months of trying to help my friend Warren Skaaren in his fight against cancer at MD Anderson had made no difference. My father's death decades ago from cancer said to me that once cancer had you in its grip, there was no escape. Lance started to cry.

I saw Lance's mother, Linda, peeking in through the kitchen door, her face pinched and pale. She looked at Lance, then at me, then back at Lance.

"I don't want to die," he sobbed.

"I don't want you to die," I said through my tears.

Later on the drive home I pulled over at Mount Bonnell, an Austin landmark that overlooks Lake Austin. I felt worthless and helpless as a friend and advisor.

Soon after that dinner together, Lance decided that Indiana was the best answer for him. It turned out to be a break that he wouldn't have had without his public announcement, without a news item, without Steven Wolff of Vanderbilt.

Four years later, in 2000, Lance was about to win his second Tour de France. I was in Paris at the George V Hotel. A small party had gathered, including the late Robin Williams. We discovered we shared nearby birthdays. I saw Robin's serious side as we talked about cancer with Craig Nichols, the oncologist who is credited with saving Lance's life. Craig explained how if you lived near one of the cancer centers of excellence in the United States, you had a better chance of survival.

Geography mattered. I thought back to when my dad contracted his cancer in our rural hometown of Three Rivers, Texas, how he died in a dark eight-room former motel that served as our local medical facility. In that moment in Paris I had an epiphany. Up to that point I hadn't felt particularly focused, despite being a founding board member of the Lance Armstrong Foundation. Suddenly I believed I had a central thing to do.

We needed an imagination session and we needed it right away, pulling together our best and brightest minds. After listening to Craig, my central thought was that we needed to find an enterprise model that would focus on helping those who didn't live in the right zip codes, those whose circumstances gave them less of a chance, those who wouldn't be giving press conferences about their cancer, those who wouldn't have saviors like Steven Wolff read their story, those unlikely to get information about the latest research.

Out of our Livestrong imagination session and great leadership by our board, staff, and volunteer community emerged the Livestrong brand with its 80 million bracelets sold (at a dollar per bracelet, a true democratization of philanthropy), over $500 million raised for cancer survivorship, the catalyzing of the Cancer Prevention & Research Institute of Texas (CPRIT) with its base funding of $3 billion over a ten-year period and a pledge of $50 million to the Dell Medical School at the University of Texas, dedicated to the transformation of health care.

My phone rang midday in January 2013. It was my friend Mark McKinnon asking me if I knew what was going to happen. Mark was asking about that night's televised interview of Lance Armstrong by Oprah Winfrey, which would be watched by tens of millions of people worldwide and which would answer long-running accusations about the use of performance-enhancing drugs. Whatever was going to happen, Mark and I didn't want to watch it alone.

I was late to Doug Ulman's house. Doug was the CEO of Livestrong. I walked in the front door at the very moment Oprah began her introduction of Lance. A small group of us sat in stunned silence as we watched. When it was over, someone asked Doug if he wanted us to leave. He nodded yes. We filed out his door quietly, got in our cars, and drove away. It was as if we hadn't watched Lance's confession of doping together, each one of us too overwhelmed to talk.

I felt as if I had been hit in the head with a hammer. I was weaving so badly as I drove on the expressway that I took the first available exit to pull over. McKinnon called. He was getting angry, the more he thought about what we had just watched. Mad that he hadn't heard anything from Lance. "Don't we deserve at least a phone call from Lance?"

"Yes," I said. I thought we did. News reports at the time mentioned that Lance had apologized to Livestrong staffers before the interview, but as far as I knew, no one on Livestrong's board had received a phone call.

I slumped in recollection of how Lance and I had met in 1993 at Quack's 43rd Street Bakery in Austin's Hyde Park neighborhood. I had started teaching in UT's Plan II program a couple of years earlier, and I scheduled regular meetings with students outside of class so that I could get to know them better. My student Bart Knaggs had brought his friend Lance Armstrong along, and I was utterly charmed by Lance's energy and his naïveté. He had asked my opinion about owning a private plane. I was opposed to private planes because of the amount of alternate good one could do with that money. Lance's look told me he thought I was nuts. I might be nuts, I thought, but what could be sillier than the idea of a bicyclist ever making any serious money. It was an amiable stalemate.

Then along came Lance's cancer, the creation of the foundation, Lance's seven Tour de France victories in a row, and then Oprah. For sure, all along there had been occasional rumors of his use of performance-enhancing drugs, rumors that I refused to believe, was determined not to believe. Now with the Oprah interview I couldn't look away anymore. And when I did my overdue homework, I learned about Lance's bullying, especially toward relatively powerless people that he tried to destroy. As I began to understand how our foundation was seen by some as an enabler of Lance's behavior, I felt ashamed, disgusted.

McKinnon was right, I think. He and many others deserved at least a phone call. Some of those who needed a phone call still break down and weep as they try to express how their lives were turned upside down by the damage done to them by Lance's actions.

What confused me that evening as I parked near the expressway exit was my inability to reconcile the devastation that had been done with the good I hoped had been accomplished. It would take time before I came to an understanding that both realities were true. The good and bad were connected, integral to one another in the messy nature of this story.

CHAPTER 15

The Reunion

When the invitation to my fiftieth Harvard Business School reunion arrived in the form of a generic email in the spring of 2017, it began, "Dear Edward." That email was followed soon by a personal handwritten invitation that began with "Dear Ed."

Those of us lucky enough to have a life wherein we are called by our middle names, in my case Lee, have a built-in advantage. We know immediately when there is a cold-call sales effort going on. The "Hi, Edward" or "Hello, Ed" exposes the hollow boilerplate sales pitch right away.

Perfect, I thought. Fifty years have gone by, and that place on the Charles River where I somehow survived the two hardest years of my life has no idea I call myself Lee. My classmate who wrote the note has no idea. While he might remember the sad hulking creature who never spoke, he doesn't remember that creature's name.

I wasn't about to return to a place where I had been so unhappy. The word "reunion" implies there once was a union that now is going to "re," but is that possible when I felt so disunited back then?

Then came another form email that said something like, "Dear Edward, Would you consider writing a 6,000-word essay about your life since graduation?" That might be interesting. Didn't some of the ideas we invented when I was serving as first president and de facto chief financial officer of Dell become case studies at Harvard Business School? I could brag about that maybe. And just because I wrote a personal essay didn't mean I had to go to the reunion. It might be useful to do a reflection essay to help me exorcise my demons about Harvard.

As I began to write, the words started tumbling out. In the weeks that followed I revised and revised the essay again. When I finished it, I felt pleased. I thought it was a well-honed essay giving a balanced account of my story over the past half century.

I walked into my study one evening to make a final decision about whether to send it. When I went to the HBS website where I had written and stored my essay, I was surprised to find the draft had disappeared. It was another blackout, except this time it was the written account of my post-HBS life story. I double- and triple-checked the site. My essay was gone, vanished, vaporized.

It was as gone as I might have been once upon a time if a 1965 blackout had occurred an hour later. Now as then, I bowed in submission and acceptance. Now as then, I went to bed to get some rest. When I awoke, I decided I had to go to the fiftieth Harvard Business School reunion.

I had to see what people looked like after fifty years, whether it was true that everything in our faces can change but never the contour of our lips when we smile. I had to walk (not run) up the stairs in Chase Hall and see if C-43 still existed. I had to find out what became of Professor John McNaughton, who must have been the savior who tipped the scale to let me graduate when others were arguing, "Hell, no."

I had to walk to the other side of the Charles River to see if the grassy knoll across from HBS was still there, the spot where I used to sit and study the place that was giving me such a hard time. I had to walk to Cambridge Common on the other side of Harvard Square (which was never a square at all) to see if the park bench was still there where I used to sit and weep far away from campus so no one would recognize me.

—◦—

I paused on the north side of the Anderson Memorial Bridge. My two years at Harvard Business School had been sheer misery. But now I was back, about to cross over the Charles River from the liberal side to where "the citadel of capitalism" awaited its graduating class of 1967.

At first glance, the business school was just as I remembered it, with its neo-Georgian architecture and lots of brick. As I crossed the bridge, I looked for the plaque that used to commemorate nineteen-year-old Quentin Compson, who had drowned himself when he was a freshman. Quentin is a central fictional character in two of William Faulkner's novels, and the smell of honeysuckle, Faulkner wrote in *The Sound and the Fury*, filled Quentin as he died.

On the other side of the bridge I walked past Chase Hall, the dormitory where Leo and Chum, my two roommates, and I lived our first year. I remembered first meeting Leo when he put his hand out to shake mine.

"Hey Boo," I said, although Leo looked nothing like Robert Duvall's Boo Radley.

"That's a line from my favorite movie," Leo said. "How did you know?"

"Lucky guess," I said as Chum put out his tiny hand.

His full name was Chumporn Nahlamlieng. He looked about four and a half feet tall and sixteen years old. Some droll spirit put our unlikely threesome together: the tallest, the shortest, and Leo, the in-between who had been the captain of Harvard's basketball team.

I already knew that neither Chum nor Leo were going to the fiftieth reunion. Chum had written in an email that he

couldn't make it. Leo Scully had died several years before. I
hadn't known that when I signed up to return and had almost
fallen out of my chair when I spotted the asterisk next to his
name as I was looking over the reunion material.

Before learning of Leo's death I had hoped that the reunion
would give us lots of time to laugh and be together and
perhaps to heal whatever needed healing. I wanted to hear
him sing again "Sweet Soul Music" in his off-key way. I didn't
know why we had lost touch. I thought we had forged a new
bond after he visited me in Austin for several days in 1987, but
we eventually lost touch again. Before I learned that he died,
I thought maybe the reunion could help us reestablish what
used to be a close friendship when we were roomies.

But I had other reasons to return. I wanted to see how my
former classmates were doing, especially my section mates (I
was in a Section B study group). And I hoped to find out more
about John McNaughton, my production management professor. He was the only teacher at Harvard who had noticed me,
saw my struggle, and helped me make it through. Back then he
seemed only about ten years older than his students, so maybe
he was still alive, well into his eighties by now. If he had passed
away, I needed to find out as much as I could about him. I
headed toward Morgan Hall, the forbidding admissions building named for iconic businessman John Pierpont Morgan, a
brick and stone building as unwelcoming as its namesake's
face. Perhaps someone there would know what became of John
McNaughton.

Inside Morgan Hall I met a young man named Eric sitting
behind a Dell computer. I wanted to tell him I used to be
Dell's first president, but I didn't. Eric asked if he could help
me, and I said I was looking for information about a professor
John McNaughton who taught production management in
1967.

Eric said that it might take a while to track down any information. I thanked him and said I was in no hurry. I checked out the books on display, which were predominantly about Harvard Business School. I looked for Duff McDonald's 2017 book *The Golden Passport,* but I didn't find it. I wasn't surprised because it expresses McDonald's belief that society today suffers from a moral failure by the MBA elite, especially Harvard MBAs, and that something went terribly wrong in the mid-1980s when money began to overpower civic values.

I looked for and found a favorite book, *Ahead of the Curve* by Philip Broughton. I had read this book a couple of times and liked it a lot. Broughton is impressed with the concept that he calls Dell's "cash conversion cycle," which is studied at Harvard as a model for how to run a business from a financial point of view. I think about how we invented that out of necessity: we only had $1,000 of capital, so we had to be ultraefficient with money. I love how academics can fancy up simple ideas with high-toned language. What Broughton dubbed "cash conversion cycle," I called "we don't spend it till we got it." At Dell we used other people's money to sustain us by having customers pay up front, keeping little to no inventory, stretching our payables to the hereafter, leasing all equipment, and taking advantage of the freebies we got from what was in those days a depressed real estate sector. In other words, we took our weaknesses and made them into a "way," and now our "way" is celebrated as a model to be studied and emulated. I put the Broughton book back on the rack where I had found it.

Eric returned and said they had no record of John McNaughton, but that sometimes their records were incomplete and I should walk over to Baker Library, which had comprehensive files on all of Harvard's past professors. Eric was worried I might get rained on because a storm was threatening, so he lent me an extra umbrella. As I departed Morgan

Hall I could see that Cash Flo's office had disappeared. The powers that be at Harvard have a way of keeping the outside shell exactly as it used to be while hollowing out the inside and replacing it with an unrecognizable, gleaming interior.

Inside Baker Library I met a man named Tim. Like Eric, Tim was also sitting behind a Dell computer. I told him I was looking for any record the library might have of John McNaughton, and soon he enlisted the aid of a woman named Rachel who asked if I was willing to wait. "As long as it takes," I said.

After about twenty minutes Rachel reported back that they had no record of John McNaughton. He was probably a visiting professor, she said, and they don't keep records of visiting professors. Her best guess was that his one-year visiting professorship just happened to coincide with my time at Harvard.

I walked outside. It had started to rain, and I unfurled the umbrella given to me by Eric in Morgan Hall. I walked past the spot where I used to dig my newspapers out of the snow before delivering them. I headed over to McCulloch Hall, where Leo, Chum, and I lived during our second year at Harvard. It now had a sophisticated card entry system near its front door. The dormitory was locked, and I couldn't get in.

I decided it was time to return to my hotel. I crossed the bridge back to the liberal side of the river and sat on the grassy bank just past the boathouse so I could get a good look at my old school. Fifty years earlier, I had sat in that same spot many times, wept a tremendous amount in despair, but never remotely considered killing myself the way Quentin did in Faulkner's novel. But I would have left Harvard had it not been for Leo and Chum's support, the help of my classmates, and the compassion of a professor Harvard had no record of.

Epilogue

In May of 1997, Jen and I were on vacation, walking an old pilgrim trail in north-central Italy. Wild pig tracks criss-crossed our pathway, a dusty winding foot trail. We threaded through the ruins of a deserted medieval castle that was put under siege in 1377. We wondered about the story behind its destruction in 1383. As we peeped through the vertical arrow slots designed for crossbows, I remembered how I used to love playing fort when I was a boy.

I looked to the west across the Tiber River from where the Etruscans had once kept watch on their rival tribe, known as the Umbrii, before the Roman Empire emerged as the dominant power. I looked to the south. Some eight miles away stood massive cloud-covered Mount Subasio. At its base was Assisi, looking like a little pink postage stamp. Once upon a time this was the home of St. Francis.

What a mistake, I thought, if we were to try to buy this ruin, a money pit. But if we didn't buy it, would we wonder the rest of our lives what might have been? Wasn't this one of the big lessons that Wayne Stark taught me, to go for the adventure?

When I was nine years old, I chanced upon a toy castle in a store window. It had the most cunning battlements and crenellated walls, complete with a drawbridge and soldiers, many armed with crossbows and pikes. Instantly I wanted that castle more than anything I had ever wanted in my life. The price was high, twenty-three dollars, and I asked my dad if he could help me get a job so I could buy the castle. Dad said he would, and soon I was working every Sunday at

Father Wogan's skeet shoot at St. Charles Borromeo Church. My job was to sit huddled in a low-slung shack and put the clay pigeons on the sling that would fling them into the air when the shooters shouted, "Pull!" The job involved some pain because I was hunched over all afternoon placing the clay pigeons. Sometimes I was too slow to pull my hand back. When the shotgun shooters yelled "Pull!" my arm would get hit by the force of the sling, leaving big bruises that I kept covered because I was determined to get that toy castle. Father Wogan, with whom I served mass every morning from the time I was in the fourth grade, usually gave me a quarter for my afternoon's work. After two years of working every other Sunday, I had earned just over thirteen dollars.

Then we moved away, and I never got my castle.

I had forgotten about that toy castle until I was stepping around the fallen stones of the Umbrian medieval ruins. I halted in my tracks as I made the long-broken connection. So that's what happens to a dream deferred. Its cost compounds interest over time.

We began the renovation of this ancient place more than twenty years ago and are still at it. There's been much work to do, especially on the restoration of the 1,000-year-old chapel. It's possible that Cimabue and Giotto, the forerunners of the Renaissance, made the eight-mile walk across the valley from Assisi around AD 1300 to paint some of the frescoes, although their work is now largely destroyed.

I try to visualize Wayne Stark's reaction to our church, named in honor of Saint Mary Magdalene. I know he would cross-examine me to extract every last detail so that his telling of the church story would be laced with juicy particulars, many of which would be embellished for maximum drama.

In those early days when we first came to Castiglione Ugolino, our place in Italy, we noticed a large tangle of bushes, wild roses, and vines that had grown within and around some kind of ruin. "I call this *la nascosta*. That means 'the hidden one,'" said our guide. The hidden one had once been a hay-rick barn where farmers kept their silage dry. The disintegrating structure was only about 500 square feet—small, but big enough on which to build something.

Luca Francia, our project manager in Italy, is a brilliant designer whom friends discovered selling hats of his own design on the main street (Corso Vanucci) of Perugia. He visited us in Texas, and once he saw our Imagination House in Austin, it was clear what we needed to do with our *nascosta*. Now it is our Italian Imagination House, with big, barn-style doors, a tall blackboard made out of slate, and wraparound views of the surrounding valley. It is where I began to scratch out my initial thoughts for this book.

For the past two years my dear friend Will Wynn has come to stay with us at Castiglione Ugolino. In his foreword to this book, Will recalls that when he met Wayne Stark many years ago, he was bombarded with stories. That was of course Wayne's stock in trade, an avalanche of stories about the adventures of the students who had gone before us.

Will has also started coming with me to the annual event in nearby Castiglion Fiorentino, where we share with the Texas A&M students details from our own stories about life at A&M, in Austin, and beyond. Will is twenty-four years younger than me, so he is the designated driver for the fifty-minute journey to Castiglion Fiorentino. I know that when I am gone, he'll continue to visit these students since he shares my feeling about the importance of keeping the gift alive we once received.

And what is the gift? I suppose it takes different forms depending on the receiver. My interpretation of the gift is that its essence encourages us to do our best to be brave, to stretch our imaginations, especially our moral imaginations, and to be in a state of deep gratitude.

When I consider gratitude, my mind goes to one of my favorite short stories, "The Mappist" by Barry Lopez. A man named Trevino has been looking for someone for many years. The object of his quest is a master mapmaker who may or may not still be alive. Trevino's task is complicated by the fact that he doesn't know the name of the person he is looking for. When chance and circumstance happen to deliver the correct name to him, it doesn't take Trevino long to connect with his man, still very much alive at age eighty-eight, living in a remote part of North Dakota.

I've loved this story from the moment I first heard it read on the radio years ago. Something about it resonated with me, no doubt because of my own search in trying to find a former teacher of mine, someone who might or might not be still alive.

Unlike Trevino, I thought I knew the name of the person I was looking for. I was wrong. His name was not John McNaughton. It had never occurred to me that maybe time had hollowed out my memory. It had never occurred to me that maybe my brain had gone a little Harvard haywire because that was such an upsetting time when I was there.

During the Harvard Business School reunion when Rachel the librarian at Baker Library had hypothesized that John McNaughton had probably been a guest professor for whom records weren't kept, I was persuaded. While there might have been a smidge of lingering doubt, I filed the matter away as case closed.

Mostly closed. More than a year later a classmate put me in touch with another classmate who suggested that maybe I had gotten the name wrong, that maybe I was really looking for someone named Curtis McLaughlin. I was incredulous because the first names were so different. However, there was a certain echoing assonance in the surnames, so I chased the

lead, which didn't take long to find on Google. I discovered
that Curtis McLaughlin was a retired professor of business
at the University of North Carolina, but I could not find any
contact information for him. I began emailing his fellow
professors at UNC. Finally, one of them knew someone who
knew someone who led me to Curtis McLaughlin.

When I called him, the voice I heard at the other end was
firm but cautious. I said I wasn't sure if he was the man I was
looking for, but when I said the year of our class, the title of
the course, and the names of some of my section mates, he
said, "Yes, Lee, I am that person."

As we talked, I learned that Curtis McLaughlin was an
eighty-six-year-old widower. I learned that Curtis spends his
days playing a little tennis, updating his textbooks, reading,
exercising, participating in discussion groups, and helping in
the governance of the continuing care retirement community
where he lives.

While he didn't remember me at all, he said, "I do read
faces. If you were in obvious distress, I would have noticed it."
He added that in those days if the teachers saw a struggling
student, they talked among themselves about what might be
done to help. And when he reminded me there had been a
faculty member named John McArthur who subsequently
became dean of Harvard Business School, my name confusion began to make a little more sense.

We talked for about forty-five minutes, about his health,
his children and grandchildren, his daily routine. Then he
said, "I almost never hear from anyone from those three years
at Harvard."

My eyes welled up. I apologized for being so late in letting
him hear from me. I wanted him to know that he had made
all the difference to me, that without him I would have been
lost and not made it through.

He paused and said, "Thank you."

Acknowledgments

Someone who has been teaching and practicing entrepreneurship as long as I accumulates a host of debts that can never be fully repaid, let alone adequately acknowledged. I want to thank some of those who have helped me over the past many decades while begging the forgiveness of those I've failed to mention.

I am grateful for all the help I've received from Texas A&M University Press, especially from Shannon Davies and her team. Readers Jimmie Killingsworth and Carlos Blanton provided me with insightful critiques of an earlier draft. Katie Duelm and Alison Tartt deftly handled the copyediting phase. Special thanks to Andy Sansom.

Alison Macor has edited my drafts, brainstormed with me, and helped keep me organized. Her talent permeates the pages of this book.

Amon Burton has been my staunch ally on so many fronts over the many decades of our friendship. Dennis Cavner is a trusted advisor I turn to again and again for counsel. Alessio Carabba is my trusted advisor and ally in Italy.

AnnaMarie Thompson provided help with early drafts. Steve Harrigan gave advice at regular intervals over too many cinnamon rolls at Upper Crust Bakery. Lydia Crooks and Lynn Merritt provided vital assistance.

Robert Jackson made the drawing for the cover of this book based on a photograph by Carol Burton. Katie Heiselberg helped with the cover.

Kim and Kenny Hill and Steve Spilker provided critical background information.

Many of the stories in this book were first written for my Chez Zee restaurant writer's group, a talented and cherished tribe that has encouraged me over many years: Stacey Abel, JoLynn Free, John Harms, Kat Jones (also the creator of the Livestrong name), Margaret Keys, Judy Myers, Bea Ann Smith, David Smith, Jen Vickers, and Sharon Watkins. Special thanks to my teachers, Elizabeth Neeld and Marie Howe.

Students attending the Texas A&M MSC summer orientation at Santa Chiara in Castiglion Fiorentino have given me invaluable feedback on early drafts over the past several summers. Without Luke Altendorf's leadership, this book wouldn't have been possible.

My students and colleagues in the Plan II Honors Program at the University of Texas at Austin are my continuing spark and delight. Special thanks to Paul Woodruff and Ronnie Earle, without whom I wouldn't have my life of teaching.

Teaching assistants are unsung heroes. I want to sing out some of mine: Anthinula Tori, Kathy Lewis, Julie Bonner Bellquist, Josh Levinson, Nikki Rowling, Tara Levy, Bart Knaggs, Emily Groth, Myfanwy Devoe, Kathy Kennedy, Tanvir Vahora, Marissa Duswalt, Sarah Andes, Ashley Crooks, Willie Cochran, Maggie Gunn, Holland Finley, Nicole Kruijs, Melissa Hall, Divya Ramamoorthy, Aarti Bhat, and Margaret Siu.

David Shiflet, John Street, and I have laughed and cried together during our supper club gatherings for the past thirty-plus years.

Westcave Preserve has been a spiritual reservoir sustaining me over the past forty years. Special thanks go to John Watson, John Ahrns, Molly Stevens, and the thousands of others who have helped rescue, support, and cherish this crown jewel of Central Texas.

My longtime assistant Kim Thrower has provided me

constant and dedicated support over our many years of working together. I am eternally grateful to her.

My family is my inspiration and joy. With love to my daughters Amanda, Suzanna, Gabriella, and Giulia; my grandchildren, Sam and Jasmine; my brothers, Frank, Tom, Bill, Kenny, and my sister Sally. In memory of my father and mother, Dallas Vincent and Thelma Ruth Walker, and my grandparents, Fred and Prudence Baker and Hugh and Eva Walker.

I especially want to thank my wife, Jen. Her love and support mean everything to me. She has done everything possible to help me in the creation of this book, and I dedicate it to her.

Index